BAGGAGE CLAIM

by Kelly Elmore

ISBN 13: 978-0-88100-173-0
ISBN10: 0-88100-173-2
Library of Congress Number: 2020938870

Cover Design by NZ Graphics

Published by National Writers Press

Library of Congress Cataloging-in-Publication Data
Elmore, Kelly
Baggage Claim by Kelly Elmore

International Standard Book Number 13: 978-0-88100-173-2
International Standard Book Number 10: 0-88100-173-0

1.   Religion/ Christian Living/ Women's Interests
2.   Religion/ Christian Living/ Inspirational
3.   Religion/ Christian Education/ Adult   I. Title
        2020938870

Dedication

I am writing this to all the women out there who have ever felt guilt, shame, unattractive, lost, ignored, insignificant, unloved, unlovable, left behind, unimportant, unworthy and so on. For all those women out there who have ever had a hole in your heart, a pain which ran so deep you felt as if you could not breathe; from losing a relationship, divorce, death, loss of dream, loss of a child (natural or adoptive), never bearing a child, abuse, and intolerance. I am asking you to please continue reading. My prayer and *hope* is this book will guide us to healing, through the knowledge and understanding that our W.O.R.T.H comes from and is found in Christ. For we are all uniquely original. We were all created by God to glorify God through our good works, according to His plan.

Contents

God's promise to us:

"Fear thou not, for I am with thee, do not be dismayed, for I am thy God; I will strengthen thee; yea, I will help thee; yea, I will uphold thee with the right hand of my righteousness."
Isaiah 41:10

CHAPTER ONE

DEPARTURE: ESCAPE PLAN

"On the first day of the week, very early in the morning, the women took the spices they had prepared and went to the tomb. They found the stone rolled away from the tomb, but when they entered they did not find the body of the Lord Jesus.
Luke 24: 1-2

"He told them; this is what is written: The messiah will suffer and rise from the dead on the third day.
Luke 24: 46

The greatest "escape" planned and executed, was the death and resurrection of Jesus. Through his death and resurrection (escape from this earth), Jesus fulfilled scripture and provided a way for us all to one day escape this earth and live with him in eternity in heaven. God put it on my heart to write a book to help other women, going through the "icky" of this world. But, how can we learn to "escape" from the icky and hold onto Christ while we are still living on this earth in our earthly bodies? We have to heal.

Our journey to healing starts with our departure, or leaving behind those past hurts, pains, and challenges and embracing what's ahead. Departure means we are leaving, usually to begin a journey, and eventually arrive at a new destination. In order to depart or leave, we need to look at *what* we need to leave behind, and why we need to escape. (We will talk more about how to escape in Chapter Four, for now we need to understand the *why* and the *what*).

"Brothers and sisters, I do not consider myself yet to have taken hold of it. But one thing I do:
"Forgetting what is behind and straining toward what is ahead, I press on toward the goal for which God has called me heavenward in Christ Jesus."
Philippians 3: 13 & 14

God is calling us, pleading with us, to forget the past and intentionally focus on what is ahead. He wants us to no longer be bound by our past, but instead to be only focused on our future in Him.

In order for us to leave our past and move forward, we must understand what is holding us back. What about our past? What happened in our past to get us where we are today, and why are we trying to escape?

Ever been in a "bad" place in your life, when every decision, every choice is the wrong or bad choice? Yep, I've been there, more than once. Let me say, it's not a fun place. In fact it can be scary. There was one choice I made which started out very scary, but ended with joy, peace, and love.

It was end of March or early April in 1991, I was 22. It was late, dark, cold, and here I am, a white girl, walking the streets of Upland, California, because the man I thought I loved, had just threatened to bash my head in with a brick. So I thought it would be safer outside than in (if anyone has ever been to Upland, you will agree, it is not a safe place, far from safe, the gangs run deep here). This man I was so in love with was hard core Crip (been shot, stabbed, in jail many times, the gang affiliation was part of his entire family, including his sister). Again, I will say I was in a bad place in my life, leading me to believe he was a good choice. So, I am walking and I stop to make a call at a pay phone (yes, pay phone ladies, remember this is back in 1991). It's a well-lit area so I walk up and call my mom, she lives in Irvine (perfectly plastic, Irvine). I was living with her because I already had one child by this "man of my dreams", and I ask her to come pick me up. She agrees, even though it is late. All I need to do is wait the 45 minutes for her to arrive, I am good, all is good, I escaped the man and my mom is coming. It's then I see three Hispanic men down the block from me talking (in Spanish) and pointing at me. To say I was scared is an extreme understatement. I was scared, shaking, and not sure what to do, where to run. There was nowhere to run, nowhere to escape, I needed to wait there for my mom, I had no more money to call her and no way to contact her to let her know I was somewhere else. So, I started calling out to God for help (I was not in relationship with God but called out to him for help). Then as the men were walking toward me, two very large Doberman's stated barking, and I mean barking, like I have never heard. They started barking so much they woke their owner, who comes outside to see what is happening. This man was an angel from God, in that moment, he saved me, and I am sure saved me from something horrible. When he walked outside and came outside of his fence with his dogs, the three men turned and walked away. He asked me if I was okay, and if I needed help. I told him I was waiting for my mom to pick me up, he then said he would wait with me until she arrived.

WOW, this complete stranger, sent by God not only came out to see what was going on, but then also stayed with me.

Oh but this is not the end, a month later I realize I am pregnant again, and feel utter discouragement. Here I was making changes to better my life. I was working (had a great job at Miller's Outpost, loved this place), I left the man who abusive, I had a car, I was paying my bills, taking care of my first child, and now I am pregnant. I was distraught. How would I ever be able to mentally or financially raise another child on my own?

I soon realized it would not be possible. So I started a search for adoptive parents, and found them. They were great, we took birthing class together, we met with the counselor together, and we bonded. I felt this was the right choice, the best thing to give both my kids a good start in life, an opportunity.

My daughter was born in December, she was small (only 5 lbs.), but healthy. I laid there in the delivery room, the nurse took her to be warmed and tested. I never in my life had ever (even to this day) felt so entirely, completely, alone. No family was with me, my sister who had brought me to the hospital had left. My daughter's parents were busy with her, and so there I was, legs in stirrups, the nurse was cleaning me, massaging my uterus. I felt like everything was happening around me, I couldn't cry, this is what I chose, so alone. I went home within hours. I could not stay there, even though they put me in a surgical bed on the surgery floor, I felt like I had to leave. Sitting in my wheelchair, in a room with a nurse and my daughter's parents, I held her, for the first and last time. I was crying so hard I could not see her face through my tears. I didn't want to let her go and at the same time knew I must. As I gave my daughter to her Mom, tears coming so fast I could not wipe them away. I knew in that moment, I was doing the "right" things, but the pain was gut wrenching, you know the kind that takes your breath away.

I cried, and cried, and cried. Some days I felt like I could not go on, like I could not breathe. So, I cried more. It felt like no one around me understood what I was going through, no one. I was so alone. I am crying now, tears streaming down my face as I remember. It was the most difficult thing I have ever done, even to this day. I cried for almost four months straight, I barely was able to take care of my first child. I was barely able to work. I saw my counselor almost daily, and if I was not in her office, I was on the phone with her, for four months. Then one day I requested to see my baby. Her mom and dad agreed, only her mom came to the visit. She was about four months old, and once I saw her, I knew, she was okay. No, she was better than okay, she was loved, and well taken care of, she was thriving. I know now I needed to see her in order to know she was good, to know my decision was truly the "right" decision. Once I knew she was good, I could move on. I was able to be at peace with my decision, I knew God was with her, and would always take care of her.

I had the benefit of proof, I was able to see my daughter was okay, and was able to let go and let God. How do we let go when we don't have proof? Well, let's start with prayer, asking God to help guide us, and to give us wisdom to know what we need to leave in our past. Leading to help us understand why we made the choices to land in a particular circumstance. We can't leave it behind if we don't understand why we chose it in the first place, otherwise we might continue to repeat our actions (which is like being a hamster going round and round on the hamster wheel). I started asking myself, why did I choose that man? Why did I go to Upland without a car? Why did I think so little of myself to walk into a gang affiliated home, where violence was "normal"? Why did I continue to have sex? My choice to go that night led to this story, to this time in my life.

Our choices and decisions, both good and bad, impact our lives. This is why it is so very important to discover the why in our choices, it's in the "why" we will find understanding, and acceptance, and ultimately the ability to leave our bad choices in the past and take the good into the future. **Our collective choices make up our past and direct our future**.

Throughout the life of Jesus he made choices, ultimately ending in the choice to die on the cross for our sin. He could have saved himself, he could have decided to not endure the pain inflicted upon him prior and during crucifixion, but he didn't. He made the choice, directing our future, to die, and in that moment take on the sin of the world. In his death, he made the ultimate choice of dying to save us while we are yet sinners.

Making the right/best choice is often hard, and we need Jesus to not only help us make decision but to give us strength to execute.

> *Our Collective Choices Make up*
>
> *Our past*
>
> *And direct our future.*

DEPARTURE: WINDOW, AISLE, OR MIDDLE

"And your ears shall hear a word behind you saying, this is the way, walk in it, when you turn to the right or when you turn to the left."
Isaiah 30:2

Decisions, decisions, decisions. For some, deciding on which seat is a big deal, for some it is always the same, and for others it is an adventure. I always try to get the window (if possible) so I can see out, look down and marvel at the world God created from nothing. Deciding on which seat to select may seem small, but what if making the choice meant living or dying? For instance, the plane crashes and you later find out, if you would have chosen the seat right behind you would have not made it. It may seem like not all decisions in life are "life or death", however, many small choices can and do add up to making the "life or death" choice. As Christians God wants us to look to Him for guidance, not relying on what our mom says, or our sister, or even our best friend, but on Him.

Making decisions without God, well, that's just cray, cray!

About 22 years ago, I did have to make a literal life and death choice. It was 1996, I was 25, recently married, and having my fourth child. I went into labor and thought: *Oh this is going to be such a breeze, number four should just come sliding out.* Boy oh boy was I wrong!

After several hours of labor I was contracting but not progressing, so the doctor came in and officially broke my water (no, I was not one of those women in movies that experiences her water breaking before full blown labor, mine was always the opposite). Then I waited several more hours before my son was finally born in the wee hours of the morning. I was so overjoyed, but the doctors took him, and I could hear someone (not sure if it was a nurse or doctor) say "he is not "pinking" up".

Well, this was not good. As a matter of fact, my son was blue/grayish. Then he was gone, whisked away, I had not even held him. *Where was he going? What is wrong?* It seemed like forever before I was in my room and someone came to talk to us (I was married to my first husband at the time). All I heard was my son had some kind of infection but they didn't know what it was, they were treating him with antibiotics. They told me to get some rest. Really? Rest? All I could think was, *I have not seen him, held him, and they want me to rest?* I was angry, I wanted answers, and I wanted to see my son.

Hours later, several doctors came into my room (just F.Y.I., if several doctors enter a hospital room, it's usually not good). My son was not improving, and they had taken him over to Children's Hospital Orange County (CHOC) hospital, Neonatal Intensive Care unit or NICU. They needed me to come, right away. I was wheeled (under the hospital) to CHOC, crying, because I could not lose another child, I just could not.

We arrive and I have to scrub my hands before I can enter the NICU. Finally I arrive at his incubator, oh my goodness, there are tubes everywhere, he is not breathing on his own, and he is almost purple, stomach distended, and I can't hold him. He is lying there, helpless, and I can't do anything.

The doctor tells us they know what's wrong; he has something called Group B strep. (GBS). This is a bacterial infection found in pregnant women, and effects about 1 in every 2000 babies. The infection causes sepsis, breathing issues, gastrointestinal and kidney problems. My son's internal organs were shutting down (liver, kidneys, etc.) We had one choice for possible life, but there was no guarantee. The doctors wanted us to choose to either put him on Extracorporeal Membrane Oxygenation or E.C.M.O. bypass or else he would for sure die. The problem was E.C.M.O. was only going to give him a 50/50 chance at survival, and the doctors could not tell us what types of effect it would have on him long term. At the time, most babies did not survive (remember this is back in 1996, and CHOC Hospital was one of two facilities in Southern California to even have an E.C.M.O. machines for babies).

What do we do? Well 50/50 was better than 100, so we decided to put him on E.C.M.O. bypass. We prayed, my church family prayed, and we waited. After 7 days (max allowed for bypass), they unhooked the E.C.M.O. machine, and we waited. He survived, the nurses even called him the "miracle baby". Not only did he live, he took to bottle feeding instantly (most babies do not take to bottle or nursing after being in the NICU for any length of time).

Today, this man is all grown up! God saved him for his purpose, he is a volunteer Firefighter, EMT and soon to be Police Officer. He is now protecting, and serving others in one of the most critically needed areas.

God's plan is just that "God's plan" not ours. Just as I chose life for my son, we too need to choose eternal life with God. We must be in relationship with God, we must pray, and ask, and God is faithful and will will provide a way, an answer. Even if the answer isn't what we think or want.

"Call to me and I will answer you; I will tell you wonderful and marvelous things that you know nothing about." Jeremiah 33:3

Here God is telling us to call out to Him, cry out to Him, when we need to know which direction to take in life. Pray, wait on God to guide us, He will always provide an answer (we may not like the answer, but God will answer). This verse promises, if we call out to God, He WILL tell us wonderful things, things we would not otherwise know. Don't go it alone, don't try to make life choices without God.

One of the most important choices we need to make is asking God to forgive us of our past choices/decisions. No matter what was in our past, no matter what decisions we made, God will forgive, always! God will use each step we take, each challenge, each trial to mold us into who He wants us to be. Let's be real clear here, I am not saying our choices do not have a consequence. They do. What I am saying is God will forgive, will always forgive, however, when we chose to live life without God (not involving Him in our decisions, denying Him, ignoring Him), and when we sin, there will be consequences. God is a gracious, loving God; He will use our consequences to shape us.

Most of us will not ever have to face a true physical "life or death" choice. But all of us will need to make a Spiritual "Life or Death choice". We know this, our choices have consequences, our choices impact others, and our choices make us who we are.

What we may think is best, most often is not what God knows is best. In the Bible I am reminded of a story about choices and how the right choice was made clear through God.

Martha and her sister Mary, two women of the Bible, were faced with a big choice, although Martha didn't understand, at least not at first. In Luke we read about how Jesus had come to a village, and Martha and Mary lived there, Martha invited Jesus in but immediately went to work preparing and cleaning, while Mary chose to sit at his feet and listen. Martha wanted Jesus to tell Mary to help her with the preparations, but Jesus said

"Martha, Martha, the Lord answered, you are worried and upset about many things, but few things are needed or indeed only one. Mary has chosen what is better and it will not be taken away." Luke 10: 38-42

Martha made a bad choice, which lead to her not spending time with God. We too make this choice all too often! Our bad choices can lead to sin. It usually starts with something small, and then leads us to something big. Be aware of the small compromises you make within yourselves. These small choices often will lead us down a long, dark road to full blown sin. It is true we all sin, and we all fall short of the glory of God. However, as we grow and mature as Christians our goal is to become more Christlike, therefore, sinning less, and serving more. Be mindful of day- to-day small choices, they can add up to danger if we are not focused on God and His plan for our life.

"If anyone hears my words but does not keep them, I do not judge that person; for I did not come to judge the world, but to save it." John 12:47

My past choices may have been "bad or wrong", but all of them lead me here, to right now, writing this book. I would not change anything. In order for me to move on back then, and now, I needed to work through my past. To understand it--the pain, the hurt, the anguish of feeling alone. I am still working on this, every day!

Understanding why we made the choices we made in the past will help us (theoretically) make better choices in the future. When we choose to involve God, before making a decision, our chances of making a good choice improve significantly.

Ladies, no matter how big or small the decisions, always remember to spend time at God's feet asking for guidance before moving forward. You will be glad you waited on God!

Don't let your sin keep you from God;
let it bring you to God.

Departure: Interruptions

"But finding no way to bring him in, because of the crowd, they went up to the roof and let him down with his bed through the tiles into the midst before Jesus."
Luke 5:19

Aww it is 9:30 p.m., kids are in bed, husband is gone on a hunting trip, the house is so wonderfully, magically, quiet. You sit in your chair (you know the chair, big, with cushions all around, holding you nice and snug). You throw your favorite blanket over your legs, and crack open THE book, the one which has been sitting, collecting dust on your nightstand for months, and you begin to read. "**MOM, MOM, MOM,**" in the silence, this cry rings out, your moment of quiet disappears into the cries of your child. Awakened by a bad dream, needing comfort from Mom, you lay down next to your child, and slowly the two of you drift off. Your night of quiet is gone, and the thought of reading THE book, slowly disappears with each breath.

As moms, wives, friends, we are often pulled away from our "plans". Sometimes this is welcoming, but what about when it's not welcoming, or maybe whatever or whoever is pulling you is irritating?

Sitting in the widow seat sounds great, most of the time, until I must use the restroom. Then I hate that I have chosen that seat, because now I am trapped, and will have to disrupt the nice woman sleeping next to me.

I am sure many of you can relate. We must get to the restroom, so we wake the person next to us and try to "slide" out. My legs are not working, my balance is off, and I fall, directly into the woman who I woke. I apologize, repeatedly, and move slowly to the restroom. Thankfully, there is no line, I finish the task and return to my seat, exhausted and wishing I had picked the aisle seat. I start thinking about how this experience mimics so much of my life. I make a choice, stumble and fall, slowly get up and complete what I started, returning to "home base" exhausted. Feeling like my choice bumped into someone else's choice, and now we are both left there, confused, irritated, and exhausted by the nonsense of our circumstance.

Life has a unique way of throwing things in our path, causing us to lose balance, and get off track. At these times it is so very important for us to seek God.

I think again, it is a choice we can make, each time, each situation. We can choose to dive in, allow ourselves to be pulled away and live. Truly LIVE in the moment, or we can choose to be bitter, and resent every second until we can leave or escape. If we can choose to live in the situation, we can find the hope and joy God intends for our lives. When we obey, when we allow God to pull away, pull us out of the "safe" place, it can be irritating. It can cause fear, but that is only because we are looking at the situation from our perspective, not God's.

> *God will bring order to our disorder through interruptions.*

Questions/ Points to Ponder

1) What areas of your life is God asking you to leave behind or let go of?

a. Before you answer, think it through, why are you holding onto them?

b. What are you getting by not letting go?

2) How can you take the first step (not all steps, remember it is a process) to let-go of things from your past?

3) How has a bad choice helped you grow in your relationship with God?

4) How can you take the first step to change how you make decisions?

5) What life interruption helped you move toward the place/plan God has for you?

CHAPTER TWO

PASSPORTS AND OTHER IDENTIFICATION: WHO AM I?

"You are altogether beautiful, my darling; there is no flaw in you"
Song of Solomon/Songs 4:7

L ife is wonderful, amazing, and at times hard, messy, and difficult. Unfortunately, some women learn at very young age to base who we are and how we feel about ourselves on what others think of us. It is based on magazine images or on how we are treated by those around us who "love" us.

I can now say at my age, I am glad I don't look like a super model. I mean, who wants to never eat, only drink water, exercise countless hours a day, end up looking like a walking skeleton, wearing redonculous- (yes, redonculous, this is one of my many made-up words, I like to use to emphasize a point) looking clothes that I would not be buried in? Nope, not me (no offence to those women out there who are super models, aspiring to be a super model, or naturally super thin and would love to gain some weight)!

Personally I want to eat ice cream, enjoy my pizza, and have a soda now and again. I felt very differently when I was younger, especially in my teen years. So, who are we? Based on worldly descriptions, maybe a mom, wife, sister, workaholic, runner, health "nut", or dare I say, Christian? How does our passport or driver's license describe us? Our passport or license describes us by height, weight. Let's all be real here, do we really want to be summed up by our driver's license or passport? Of course, not. We actually have contests to see whose picture is the worst. I truly think the DMV tries to take bad photos on purpose and they sit in the back at the end of each day and laugh out loud at the pictures. But, who are we? I know we are more than our physical being.

As a child I was raised in the Nazarene Church. I attended most Sundays; I was even baptized in the Church "pool". Then my world started to crumble, I was seven and my parents were getting a divorce. I was the middle child (at the time), very awkward, I wore glasses, red hair, freckles, my teeth were in bad shape, and I had a very obvious overbite from sucking my thumb. I would say I was the "ugly duckling". My parent's divorce affected me so deeply, I had to repeat second grade.

Let's fast forward to the ever wonderful, teen years, umm, not so wonderful for me. I am a freshman in high school, is there anything worse? I am a year older than all my other class mates (due to repeating second grade) and I am more developed physically then other girls my age. The boys were terrible, they called me all kinds of not so nice names, teased me about my rear-end, my hips, my breasts, my hair, my glasses, basically every physical attribute was scrutinized. I started to look at myself as fat and ugly, a girl no man would want. To compound matters, my father had also basically disappeared after the divorce. He would come to pick me and my siblings up when he could, but was never consistent, and most of the time we lived with my mom and stepdad.

My Dad abandoned me. The boys at school mocked me. My stepdad was physically and verbally abusing my little brother, and I was powerless to help. I felt alone, abandoned, and ugly. I thought maybe if I lost weight my dad would love me enough to come see me, or the boys at school would stop teasing me.

I allowed the world and people around me to define who I was and how I felt. This method of thinking took me down a very dark path, wrought with pain, anger, and bitterness. I lost touch with God and began to sink. Where was God now? I am drowning and no one helped.

I started dieting and exercising. I began to lose weight, however, I still saw myself as fat and ugly. So I continued to lose weight, I stopped eating, and worked out whenever I could. I remember one day I was riding my bike (oh yes, this ages me because kids today don't ride bikes) and I fainted, right there on the street, fainted and fell off my bike. My mom took me to the doctor. He said it was a phase and I would be okay, to just leave me be and I would eventually start eating again. He was wrong, I didn't start eating, and one night I'd had enough. Where was God, why didn't He come help me? I wanted to stop feeling, I wanted to stop hurting, stop my stepdad from hurting my brother, stop crying, stop everything. I attempted suicide.

I don't remember who found me, all I remember is it was not what I thought, at all. I took pills and thought I would fall asleep and never wake. That is not even close to what happened. I was vomiting for hours, I passed out. I woke in the hospital with tubes down my nose, and doctors forcing charcoal down my throat. It was awful. A few days later my Dad came to see me. I was so excited. My Dad was there. He came to see ME! For the first time in a long time I felt loved, special, wanted.

All of us women long to be loved by our Dads and I was no different. Unfortunately, his attention did not last, and I was again left feeling unwanted. I took this into my adulthood along with the longing to feel loved, wanted, accepted, and special. We seek these worldly methods only to be lead down the wrong road, and we make decisions, bad decisions, grasping at anything to help us feel better. In the process of grasping at anything to make us feel better, we lose sight of being a child of God and only see what the world sees. God is this only one who can give us true unconditional love, make us feel wanted and accepted, and be our ever present light. *What I didn't know then was God was with me. He is still with me, because He chose me.*

What I needed to learn (listen ladies this took me a very long time), was my beauty came from the inside and that is what matters most. Once I realized my beauty came from within me, not from the outer shell (my body), I was able to reflect beauty out, allowing me to see my beauty and for others to see God's love through my inner self. Our inner beauty starts with accepting and receiving our worth through the blood Jesus shed on the cross for us. Through his pouring out of love we find our worth. We can embrace our identity found in Christ. We are daughters of the King! Our worth comes from His great love of us, so much so, He sent His only Son to die on the cross for every one of us. Yet even though we were sinners He loved us enough to die for us. Embrace your worth and identity found only in God the Father.

> *What I didn't know then was God was with me,*
> *He is still with me, because*
> *He chose me.*

Passports and other Identification: Identity in Christ

"He said to her, Daughter, your faith has healed you. Go in peace and be freed from your suffering."
Mark 5:34

<u>God chose us</u>, He invited us to be His children. Wow, let that sink in, and He invited us, and picked us out on purpose to be part of His family. We are loved, wanted, chosen by the one true God, who created us from nothing, then gave us the right to be His children.

How much more weight should we give to what God's feels about us than the world? When the world strips away our identity, leaving us empty, lost, alone, and wondering "who am I?"

We can answer back with "I am a child of God", loved, wanted, chosen, and set apart for His work.

"Yet to all who did receive him, to those who believed in his name he gave the right to become children of God. Children born not of natural decent, nor of human decision, or a husband's will, but born of God." John 1:12 & 13

Say that out loud: "I am a child of God. I am loved. I am wanted, and I am chosen. I am set-apart."

"But we ought always to thank God for you, brothers and sisters loved by the Lord, because God chose you as first fruits, to be saved through the sanctifying work of the Spirit and through belief in truth." John 2:13

Sanctifying or sanctification is being eternally set-apart for Yahweh (God), and can only happen through God, as he is the only one to cleanse our hearts to prepare us for His work. Through His cleansing, He delivers us from the darkness of this world. He releases us from worldly opinion and description, stripping us down to simply be a child of the one true God.

Our identity is found in Christ, our passport to heaven has already been stamped with the blood of Christ, He has already paid for our ticket, it is up to us to discard our old identity and grab onto God's rescue ring buoy. Don't let go! Always remember we belong to God, we are who He says we are, and He won't let us drown.

> *Our identity is found in Christ, our passport to heaven has already been stamped with the blood of Christ, he has already paid for our ticket, it is up to us to discard our old identity and grab onto God's rescue ring buoy, don't let go!*

Questions and points to Ponder

1) How does knowing God chose you, knowing God loved you even before you were formed, change how you see yourself?

2) Who were you before Christ, and what has changed through embracing the idea that God adopted you into his family?

3) How does being a daughter of the King change what others see in you?

4) How does being the daughter of Christ change how you see others?

CHAPTER THREE

MEAL AND DRINK SERVICE: FAILED EXPECTATIONS

"Waiting for our blessed hope, the appearing of the glory of our great God and Savior Jesus Christ, who gave himself for us to redeem us from all lawlessness and to purify for himself a people for his own possession who are zealous for good works." Titus 2:13-14

I am going to age myself with this one, remember back in the day when we could pre-order a meal on certain (longer) flights? Now we are lucky to get a bag of aged nuts or pretzels, or for a small fee (a week's pay) we can choose to have a box "meal" and I use the term "meal" loosely. It's not really a meal, it's more of a snack, but we pay as if we are eating a five star dinner. Oh, but back in the day, we could get an actual meal. Although both the box "meal" and the real "meal" from way back contained food, we were often still left feeling like something was missing; it just was not what we expected the "meal" to be. We expect to get something wonderful to eat (due to price), and we end up with something which resembles a meal but falls short of our expectations. This is usually quickly and easily resolved once we land, we can indulge in some local dish which covers our disappointment from our flight meal, and allows us to move on to enjoy our time away without thinking again of the failed food expectation. However, in life, it usually not this simple.

Failed life expectations often cause deep wounds and hurt which paralyze us, leaving us feeling angry, bitter, disappointed, and alone. Let's face it, we can't avoid failed expectations. We are human and we will fail ourselves and others. It's truly unavoidable. No matter if the failed expectation is from something small like failed diet and/or exercise program, or experiencing the failed expectation of a "happily ever after" through the devastating loss of a spouse or child. These can cause such internal damage, it can be hard to recover.

Our one true source of hope is Jesus. We will talk more later in the Turbulence chapters about allowing God to heal us. For now, I want to talk about what happens to us (internally) when we experience failed expectation and how we can learn to lean into Jesus for our comfort and peace.

"The LORD is my rock, and my fortress, and my deliverer; my God, my strength, in whom I will trust; my buckler, and the horn of my salvation, and my high tower."
Psalms 18:2

Failed life expectations cause anger, bitterness, and disappointment. This is because we expect something, but end up with something totally different, causing great distress. We get angry and bitter because life is supposed to be "happily ever after" right? So what do we do when our "happily ever after" changes? We are supposed to be married forever, but there is a staggering rate of divorce and death of a spouse. As women, we are made to have children, so why can't some women conceive? Those of us who do have children, expect we will pass before them, but what about when death happens in the reverse order, or if our child becomes dependent upon drugs/alcohol? We work our entire lives building a home only to have a hurricane (literal and metaphorical) hit us and leave us devastated.

One of my friends was "coaching" me about my failed expectation of God's timing. I was complaining about not having a spouse, being lonely, and basically having a pity party and she asked me what my favorite cookie was. Of course, hands down my favorite cookie is a double stuff Oreo! There is nothing better. I can almost taste one now, I image myself grabbing a couple from the package (okay, okay, I grab more like four but who is counting). Get myself some ice cold milk, and dunk the first cookie, just for a few seconds or long enough to get the outer chocolate cookie a little mushy, but not all the way mushy. Oh, I take the first bite, **yes**, almost heaven, truly, almost heaven here on earth. Then I grab the next cookie, take another bite, but this time, instead of a bite with mushy outside and creamy inside, I get crunchy outside, and it's not heaven this time, it's crunchy! I have to dunk it again to get the outside fully mushy, aww there we go, better.

Although life is much more serious, we still experience the same disappointment, maybe even anger when we take a bite and expect to get mushy/creamy bliss and instead we get crunchy/creamy, and we didn't want or ask for crunchy/creamy, we expected mushy/creamy. With the cookie there was an easy "fix" but in life, it's not so easy. Kind of like the saying "When life gives you lemons, make sweet lemonade".

Expectations are tricky, they change and increase as we age. One thing I know for sure, we have all experienced failed expectations, and when this happens we have all

31

been hurt, and disappointed. Anger, bitterness, hurt, and disappointment from failed expectation can cause memory overload, and possibly lead us down a dark road trying to get back to our "happily ever after" . But without Jesus, "happily ever after" is just not possible in this world. We can't place our happily ever after in things of this world, our true happily ever after is with God, and only God, because we are human and we will fail.

So what do we do when we get the opposite of what we want, when our expectations are not met? We lean into Jesus. Many times in life we *think* we want the mushy/creamy cookie, but God knows what we need, and he is able to provide for our needs. What I learned from the cookie story is this, sometimes the memory or the anticipation of the cookie was driving me to think I wanted the cookie, but the reality of eating the cookie could fail my expectation of what the cookie would taste like. Sometimes I got the marvelous, mushy/creamy and sometimes I got the crunchy. *Understanding what we want can get clouded by the memory of something in our past we thought was perfect.*

Are you ladies familiar with the Jonah and the whale story? Well this is it (summary version); God called to Jonah one day and told him to go preach to Nineveh because the people were very wicked. Jonah hated this idea because Nineveh was one of Israel's greatest enemies. Jonah wanted nothing to do with preaching to them!

Jonah tried to run away from God in the opposite direction of Nineveh, and headed by boat to Tarsish. God sent a great storm upon the ship and the men decided Jonah was to blame so they threw him overboard. As soon as they tossed Jonah in the water, the storm stopped.

God sent a whale to swallow Jonah and to save him from drowning. While in the belly of the whale, Jonah prayed to God for help, repented, and praised God. For three days Jonah sat in the belly of the fish. Then, God had the whale throw up Jonah onto the shores of Nineveh.

We can see failed expectation in this biblical story too. Jonah had the expectation of *not* going to Nineveh, for the simple fact that he didn't want to. This expectation was a total failure. He ultimately ended up right where God told him to go, by way of a whale! Can you imagine being Jonah, thinking you are "getting away" from God by trying to sail away only to end up in the belly of a whale and basically vomited up on the shore of Nineveh? Talk about failed expectation. God dealt with Jonah's disobedience and Jonah ultimately repented and went onto do the work God called him to do. Initially Jonah tried to run and hide, because he did not want to go. One other thing this story tells us, even when our expectations fail and we try to go our own way to feel better, God will not let us go! Although our expectations fail, God always knows what is going to happen in our lives. Therefore, we need to lean into him during these times for guidance and direction.

God showed me through the cookie metaphor, and through Jonah and the Whale, to trust and cling to him. While waiting for Him to send me my future husband, I needed to concentrate on serving God and others, and not on the memory or anticipation of only the good parts of what marriage brings, but also the hard/tough parts of what marriage really involves.

I want us to all grasp the truth of God, the promises of God and hold these tight. Write them on your heart, so when we experience a failed expectation we don't hang onto our anger, bitterness, and disappointment. Instead we allow ourselves to feel the hurt/sting of the harsh reality of life and then we let go of the hurt, pain, anger, bitterness, and disappointment making room for love, patience, kindness, and God's goodness.

When things or people in this life fail us or we fail ourselves, we can't turn to the world for healing, I urge us all to turn to God for comfort, healing, and true restoration.

Understanding what we want can get clouded by the memory of something in our past we thought was perfect.

MEAL AND DRINK SERVICE: FAILED EXPECTATIONS

PART TWO

"Yes, my soul, find rest in God; my hope comes from him. My savior, my high tower, my refuge, my rock and my fortress, I will not be shaken."
Psalms 62: 5 & 6

What a day! How many times do we say this? I say it all the time. I am a single parent (raising a teenage boy). I work full time, I volunteer at church, I am starting a woman's ministry, and writing this book. To say I am busy is an understatement. I don't list these things to make myself "sound/look" like a great Christian. I list them to convey how much I need God in my every day, you know the day to day "life" stuff.

Day to day life can be hard, challenging, busy, and down right disappointing! Where is the love? Seriously, have any of us ever felt like, I am "doing" all the right Christian things (going to church, leading or being in a life group, praying, reading the Bible, and so on) but my life is always such a mess. Why isn't God blessing me? Doesn't God see all this stuff I am doing, where is the love? I deserve to have an easier life, or at the very least, I should get something for all my effort.

I have struggled with this "deserving" concept for a while now. Once I really started devoting my life to God, going on mission trips, starting my ministry, I thought for sure; "now my life will get easier because I am obeying God, now I will get something for my effort."

The most wonderful reality is this, ladies, God does not give us what we deserve, this is called grace. And God gives us what we DON'T deserve, this is called mercy. This can be difficult to grasp so let's think of it like wheat grass vs. candy.

Our human way of thinking focuses on self. God's thinking focuses on others. If we think we deserve because of something WE have done, we are way off, even if the something was for someone else. This is because WE don't do anything except what God allows and calls us to do, therefore, it is His GRACE (not giving us what we deserve, which is punishment for our sins) and MERCY (giving us forgiveness and eternal life, what we don't deserve). No matter what we ever do on this earth, NOTHING will change God's love of us. NOTHING will change how much God to bless our lives. Nothing we do or don't do will change God's ability to pour out His grace and mercy upon us, daily. Therefore, God doesn't give us wheat grass (what we deserve, icky) he gives us candy (what we don't deserve, yummy), even though we don't deserve the candy He freely gives it to us. We can have a piece or more every day. God's grace and mercy are endless!

I know it can be hard to stay positive, daily life can bring us to our knees. Let's face it, we will drop our brand-new phone, shattering the screen, five minutes after purchase. Or get a flat tire on the way to the job interview, or lose our car keys, or "fill in the blank". Any number of life challenges are thrown at us every day. Some are small, like dropping your favorite bagel with cream cheese on the floor, and some are big, like losing a loved one or being told you have cancer, or losing your job.

> *God does not give us what we deserve, this is called grace. God gives us what we don't deserve, this is called mercy.*

Life is full of disappointments, so how can we stay positive? How can we live in joy and not in sadness and despair? I wish the answer were simple, like "do this" every day and poof, you now have joy. I am finding it's not easy at all to stay joyful in times of disappointment, it is downright hard!

I bought a house, it was a nice house, on two and a half acres, trees out front, basement, three bedrooms, nice home. When I moved in I naturally expected this house to function, meaning, I expected the electric to work and the heat to come on and the plumbing to flow. Boy did I have a false expectations!!

After living in the house for about two years, I started to have plumbing issues. The first one was septic related (for those readers who might not know what septic is, well, it's the sewer for country living). So, imagine this, I need to do laundry, so I gather my stuff, head downstairs and I smell something awful, so I set the dirt cloths down and start to investigate. It did not take long to locate where the smell was coming from. My septic had backed-up and I had sewage in my basement. Seriously, I think this was the most disgusting thing EVER! I have changed many a diaper, but this was no diaper!

I get the mess cleaned up, pulled up carpet which had been ruined, and hope it does not happen again. Well, it does happen again, a few months later. This time no sewage, this time water from using the washing machine was flooding the basement. The septic man came out, told me and my son what to do so that this doesn't happen again. Again, I am hopeful we can avoid another disaster in the basement. Not so fast, next a series of events happen, one of the pipes starts leaking, another flood occurs. Then the toilet in my upstairs, main bathroom starts to leak, causing a large hole in the basement ceiling. Called the plumber, it was fixed. Then it starts leaking again, called the plumber back, he fixes something else. Then my master bathroom toilet starts leaking, had to have the plumber come out twice for this one too. There were three large holes in the basement ceiling, all caused by leaks. All had to be fixed, more than once before they were "totally" fixed, without leaking.

Don't the circumstances in our lives often feel like leaky plumbing? Like there is a constant drip, drip, drip of disappointment, which begs for fixing but we can't get the drip plugged? Sisters, life is full of constant, slow drips of disappointments flooding our world, causing large, gaping holes which are desperately in need of repair.

I wish I could say we can somehow stop the slow drip of disappointment, but we can't. Life is life, it's how we chose to deal with the drips which matters. We can choose to let the drips flood our spirit out or we can choose to call out to God to be our life saver, to pull us from the flooding waters of disappointment onto the shores filled with grace and mercy. Through His grace and mercy, we will find joy. Joy to fill us, allowing us to live in joy even though we are walking through the valley.

I know we all have disappointment in our lives and we all handle disappointment differently. Before committing my life to Christ, I dealt with disappointment as a personal attack, like someone or something in the universe had it in for me. I think it is easy to get sucked back into thinking like this, to take circumstance personally. If we peel back the layers, we might see, disappointment is not a personal attack, no one is out to get us (well, except Satan). The truth is, life happens. Plans are broken, relationships fail, people leave us, people die, every disappointment is another "heart concussion".

A concussion is when the brain is injured, and the brain itself "sloshes" (see use of my fast-medical prowess) around in the skull with enough force to cause loss of "normal" brain function, and may also cause bruising or bleeding. It can cause someone to feel sluggish, nauseous, have a headache, dizzy, confused, and basically feel "not normal". In the same way, disappointment might cause someone to experience a "heart concussion", leaving them feeling confused, depressed, and "not normal".

Can you imagine the disappointment Jesus felt when Judas betrayed Him, and Peter denied Him? I know we feel disappointment, but Judas and Peter not only disappointed Jesus, they betrayed Him! I know, it was all part of God's plan, right?

Every time we experience disappointment our heart is "sloshed" around and bruised. Like a brain concussion, we need time to heal, and to heal we need to unplug (leave our TV, phone, computers) and rest with God.

So, why do we get do hurt when we are disappointed? It's God plan so we should be joyful, correct?

Listen ladies, ya' all know by now, and I will always be the first to admit, I am not joyful when my phone cracks, or when my son is failing Literature & Composition. No honey, I am far from joyful. I do think God understands our feelings. It is okay to feel, He made us with feeling, so go ahead, give yourself permission to feel. I simply ask, don't allow yourself to stay in that anger, or pity, or sadness. Feel, and then go talk to God.

I had started a new position at work. As usual, I wanted to do my best, put my best foot forward. I wanted to help, to make things better. I quickly figured out my boss and I had very different ideas of what "help" meant, and what the definition of success looked like. Look, I am almost 50 and I have been doing the same type of work almost my entire life. I have always had "exceptional" reviews, but now, I felt like a failure, every, single, day! Nothing I created, nothing I did was ever good enough or satisfied my new boss. I wanted to quit.

Oh, but I could not quit. I am a single parent, I must provide for my son. So, I didn't quit, but I did cry. I cried so much my shirt had tear stains! That's a lot of crying! Then two of my co-workers (whom I had told I wanted to quit) both encouraged me and listened to my gripes, then both told me to pray.

I know many of us feel like crying, daily. Maybe because our toddler kept us up all night with vomiting, or our husband forgot to take the trash out, the pregnancy test says no (again), your child is arrested, or your boss tells you the company is down-sizing and you are no longer needed. Sometimes we experience larger than life disappointments, sometimes the disappointment is small, either way, we are left with a "heart concussion" and we need time to heal before the next disappointment hits us, and believe me ladies, there is another one around the corner.

One of the best ways to heal my heart is to stop, drop, and pray. I know, it may sound silly, but it truly does help. Just say a quick, simple prayer, ask God to soften the blow of disappointment, ask God to help us not take everything personal, ask God to give us peace and forgive our sin.

"If my people, who are called by my name, will humble themselves and pray and seek my face and turn from their wicked ways, then I will hear from heaven, and I will forgive their sin and will heal their land".
2 Chronicles 7:14

God gives direction to us, we simply need to seek Him!

When we wholeheartedly seek God, He will answer us. He will save us. Hold tight to His promise to never leave us, to always guide us, and to be our hope.

"You will seek me and find me when you seek me with all your heart."
Jeremiah 29:13

Life is full of disappointments. This won't ever change, not while we are on this earth. *How we chose to handle the disappointments will impact our daily attitude and our daily attitude will determine where we allow God to take us in life.*

Jesus experienced disappointment too. Greater disappointment than we could ever imagine, and he too cried out to God to help him, so must we cry out to our Father to help us.

Stay the course, don't give up, with every valley there must be a mountain.

41

MEAL AND DRINK SERVICE: BREAD OF LIFE

"Then the LORD said to Moses, Behold, I am about to rain bread from heaven for you, and the people shall go out and gather a day's portion every day, that I may test them, whether they will walk in my law or not."
Exodus 16:4

When the Israelites were walking in the Desert of Sin (between Elim and Sinai) after leaving Egypt, they expected God to provide for them. They expected God to save them, as He had done by parting the Red Sea, they had big, larger than life expectations. However, these expectations drove the Israelites to complain to Moses and Aaron about God's lack of provision.

God heard them and responded to Moses, telling Moses to have the people go out each day to collect the manna and quail, but to only collect enough for a day. They didn't need to grab more than they needed for a day, God wanted the Israelites to trust him. But they began to grumble again. They began to complain about only having manna and quail to eat. Even though God was providing for them, even though God had brought them out of Egypt they still didn't trust Him, They still didn't accept all God had done. The

Israelites expected a T-Bone and got manna/quail. Oh, they were missing the point.

When we expect to receive anything from God, we have already lost our focus. As we discussed earlier, God doesn't give us what we deserve, he gives us what we don't deserve. This was true of the Israelites too. He gave them food, even though they didn't trust Him. But what God truly wants us all to understand, is He is our bread of life, He is all we need.

He will provide for us, He already has. He sent his son to die for us, forgiving our sin and making an eternal home in heaven. How quickly we forget all he has done for each of us. Just like the Israelites, God saves us, and we forget. God saves us, and we forget. Repeatedly, God continues to provide, and we continue to forget.

It is so easy to forget what God has done. To help myself remember I write down my answered prayers, and the moments in my life I know God has moved mountains. I post these on my prayer wall, so I can remind myself, in my dark times, in my challenging times of God's goodness. I remind myself of all God had already done for me, urging me to trust Him, urging me to believe He will be with me no matter what I am facing.

It may seem I have some pretty big mountains God has moved in my life, so it would be easy for me to always trust, to always remember what God has done. But the truth is, I struggle just as much as everyone does. I need to be reminded of God's goodness. I also need to remind myself that no matter what I expect will happen, no matter how much I want something to happen, God's plan is always better. God will always provide. So why do we forget, why do we need constant remainders of God's goodness?

The usual suspect here is Satan, he will tell you lies. He will dangle your failed expectations in front of you, like a blinking billboard sign. Telling us God was able to move this mountain, telling us God didn't care, because we don't deserve it, or because we are not good enough. All the usual lies Satan tries to tell us, all the ways Satan tries to lead us away from God. Satan will try to tell you because this failed, we will always fail.

In these times, we must recall what God has done. This so important, always have reminders posted, so when Satan tries to take a failed expectation and twist it all around into a lie, turn it round on him. Show him God is in control. He will always provide. He will always give us new hope for He is the bread of life.

Questions and Points to Ponder

1) What is recent failed expectation?

    a.   Why do you think your expectations failed?

2) How can changing your way of thinking change your expectation?

3) What is an example of God's Grace and Mercy in your life?

4) What are some things (slow drips) in your life that will cause large damage if not healed (fixed)?

5) What is a recent incident which caused a "heart concussion" and how did you heal from it?

CHAPTER FOUR

TURBULENCE: FEAR

*"And so, we know and rely on the love God has for us.
God is love. Whoever live in love lives in God, and God in
them. This is how love is made complete among us so that
we will have confidence on the day of judgment: In this
world we are like Jesus. There is no fear in love. But
perfect love drives out fear, because fear has to do with
punishment. The one who fears is not made perfect in
love."*
1 John 4: 16-18

Once on the plane one of the first signs seen is "Fasten
seat belt" which is followed by instructions. Please
remain in your seats with your seat belt securely
fastened. Wouldn't it be nice if all challenges or trials came with
a warning? "Hold on, life is about to get rough." The rough
patch may be self-inflicted or a pruning from God, either way,
we don't get warnings. How then do we prepare for life's
battles? How can we keep moving when our lives turn upside
down?

First, we must understand this: everyone experiences
challenges, tests, and trials. We are not alone! God is always

with us; he will never leave us or forsake us. Let's look at Abram and Sarai (later God renamed them to Abraham and Sarah).

Abram was given a promise from God. God promised Abram he would make him into a great nation, and Abram's offspring would be given land. *"After this the word of the Lord came to Abram in a vision: Do not be afraid Abram, I am your shield your great reward."* This is a promise God has given to us, we should not be afraid, for he is our shield and our great reward. But Abram and Sarai didn't listen, they were fearful and thought God needed help fulfilling his promise to give Abram's offspring this new land. Since Sarai had not conceived, Abram and Sarai crafted their plan to help God out. I don't know about you, but I too have thought God needed my help, and tried to intervene and "make things happen" because God was not moving fast enough. I was losing hope God would be able to fulfill his promise.

Abram ultimately slept with his slave Hagar, who bore him a son, Ishmael. God did not condemn Abram, instead he created a new covenant with him and Sarai. He changed their names to Abraham and Sarah, Sarah had a son when Abraham was 100 and Sarah was 90, his name was Isaac. Abraham and Sarah lost hope, they became fearful, and did not understand how God was going to fulfill his promise. I know we all have gone through trials where we don't see a way out. It looks impossible, but with God all things are possible. His timing is always perfect, never too early or too late, instead always right on God time. When God's timing does not match ours, we can rest in his grace, knowing he is our shield and our great reward. Even when we can't see a way, there is a way, its God's way.

God has also given us "angels" on earth, to help support us and encourage us. Satan will try to tell us we are not strong enough, or no one will understand your situation, or he will try and tell us we are dirty/shameful, and that God will not forgive us.

Many times in life the challenges I have faced were self-inflicted. Meaning, I caused my situation, due to bad decisions or choices, all because I was not seeking God. I don't know about you, but I am famous for making a decision based on fear. The fear of being alone, fear of losing, fear of being too old, too fat, fear of not being loved and wanted, has caused me to settle for someone less-than, someone other than the man God chose for me.

Fear is one of Satan's greatest tools; he uses fear to keep us from moving. Satan uses fear to fill our world with turbulence, to try and get us to lose focus on God. *When we allow Satan to keep us in fear, we are not living the life God called us to live.*

"For the Spirit God gave us does not make us timid, but gives us power, love, self-discipline." 2 Timothy 1: 7

Fear is like a snow ball. Fear starts out small (Satan does this on purpose, because we tend to ignore the tiny fears). Like a snowball rolling down a hill at high speed, we can see the ball begin to grow, increase in strength, and speed and before we know if the snow ball overpowers us. Fear works the same way. If we choose to not confront and deal with the fear in the beginning when it is small, a "fear ball" begins to form, and it grows, increases in strength, and speed, eventually crashing into us and leaving us feeling powerless against it. But wait, that is not the end, this is a trick Satan will use to disarm us, so he can continue his attack on our lives. I understand tackling fear is brave, and we should not try to do this alone, like a warning label, God has already helped guide us to where our help comes from, no matter if we face the fear when it is small or if it is a giant. Ladies, when the time comes to stand and face your fear, first put on the full armor of God, and prepare for battle. No longer allowing the fear ball to grow and over power.

"Put one whole armor of God, that you may be able to stand against the wiles of the devil."
Ephesians 6:11
> ➤ Belt of Truth
> ➤ Breastplate of Righteousness
> ➤ Shoes of Peace
> ➤ Shield of Faith
> ➤ Helmet of Salvation
> ➤ Sword of the Spirit

I have been in many relationships, and was married twice. I was always in a relationship or looking for a relationship. You know how it is, going from one bad relationship to another looking for the special "someone". None of my relationships were very good, some better than others, but none of them were great. Neither one of my marriages were to the right man, or God's choice for me. I married because I was afraid. I married someone who didn't love me because I didn't feel worthy of love, not true love, that was only for other girls. I was in the business of having relationships based on the other person needing me (usually financially), but never loving me.

My fear of not being loved made me settle for someone less-than God's best. I felt I did not deserve God's best. I felt I was not worthy of God's best (we will talk more about this later). Again, Satan lying to me telling me this is all you get, take him because there is no one else who is going to love you, he is as good as you will get. Satan's lies run deep and he makes them sound soooooo good. Be careful of what you think you hear. I thought for sure God had brought me this wonderful man, he went to the same high school as I did, we were Christian's, he had a son with a name almost the same as my son's, our last names were even the same. Sigh, he was not the man God had for me. I chose to only see and hear what I wanted to hear (again, I caused my own challenge). I was not listening to God, I was not paying attention to the warming signs from the Holy Spirit. Satan made this man "appear" so great, but he was not. Fear of being alone drove me listen to Satan's lies, and into the arms of a man who was not from God, who was not for me. Fear causes us to stumble, and because we are human we often resort to self-medication to help feel better. Instead of turning to God, we turn to worldly methods to feel "good." Our fear drives us to make choices for others instead of God.

In 1 Samuel 15 Saul was commanded by God, to wipe out the Amalekites (killing every man, women, child, calf, lamb, sheep). Saul went into battle but spared the king Agag and the finest calves and sheep for sacrifice (which God did not ask of him). When Samuel heard of what Saul did, he was upset and asked him why he didn't follow God's command. Saul replied, he was fearful of his men, so he gave into them. I know I am guilty of giving in to others, you know peer pressure. Doing something we know is wrong but doing it anyway, so others think we are "cool".

Saul did the same thing, he went against God's command and was ultimately removed as King. Sisters don't let your fear of not belonging, or not being "cool" drive us to not follow God. God wants our obedience above our "coolness". We need to make sure we are following God's commands and not the world.

Fear is disguised by what we THINK looks good and appears to be from God, but ladies, Satan is alive, and he is seeking to devour us. Satan does not want us to get what God has for us, so he will constantly be there trying to trick us and choose that which is not of God or from God.

Make sure to keep your focus on God, if something is too good to be true, pray, and God will answer. It may not be what we want to hear, but God will answer and give us clarity. Be in the Bible, every single day! As often as you can, God will use his written words to provide a path. He is our light in the darkness, call upon him. In his perfect love, there is no fear. For God is love.

When we allow Satan
To keep us in fear,
We are not living
The life God
Called us to live.

TURBULENCE: SELF-MEDICATING

"Then Samson prayed to the Lord, Sovereign LORD, remember me. Please God strengthen me just once more and let me with one blow get revenge on the Philistines for my two eyes. Then Samson reach out toward the two central pillars on which the temple stood, bracing himself against them, his right hand on one, his left on the other. Samson said. Let me die with the Philistines. Then he pushed with all his might and down came the temple on the rules and all the people in it. Thus, he killed many more when he died then while he lived."
Judges 16: 28-30

Self- medication is a dangerous and slippery slope. I struggle with self-medication all the time. I want to feel good, and I want to feel nothing all at the same time. I think back to Samson, and God gifted this man with super strength, and he was nice on the eyes too. Samson used his gift to try and help people (at least he did in the beginning). Samson was unsettled, unfulfilled, and was in search of validation. He started using his strength and good looks to fulfil his own desires and needs. He started self-medicating through concurring people, and seeking sexual pleasure. This would ultimately lead to his downfall. He met and became obsessed with Delilah. Satan used this desire to try and destroy Samson. But God still wanted to use him, even after he turned away from God, God still loved him and used him. In the end Samson lost his strength (when his hair was cut), his sight, and was put in prison. It was then Samson returned to God, in his dying breath, gave God glory and praise, and called upon God to help him one last time. God did!

God loves us! Even when we can't feel his love it is there. This world brings us challenges, and we can lose sight of God's love for us and like Samson, we may even turn from God and try to make ourselves feel better. Through sex, drugs, alcohol, shopping, food, and so on, the list of ways we self-medicate are as vast as gains of sand. There is a way to stop self-medication, all we need to do is call out to our God. He is there, waiting for us.

One of the things I used for self-medication started out innocently enough, but quickly became much more. I started running, yes ladies, running. I ran half-marathons and one full marathon. When I was running I could cope with a failing marriage, low self-esteem, stress, and financial issues. When I ran I could handle anything. Or so I thought. Has anyone else out there thought they had it all together? All figured out? Then, WHAM, from out of nowhere, we are taken down, in an instant our life changes?

This was me, except I was literally hit, while running and ironically the song "No more Drama" was playing.

In an instant my world was changed forever, my life as I knew it was taken from me, without a "fasten your seat belt" warning.

By the grace of God, I survived a hit and run. The accident left both of my legs broken at the ankle. I would not walk, much less run. As I recovered, I became aware my left ankle was severely damaged, limiting my movement and causing constant pain. I was so thankful to be alive, to be able to walk, I was at peace about what had happened to me.

I was not aware at the time, but this accident completely changed the trajectory of my life. I was always a Christian, but this accident made me trust in God. Pushing my relationship with Him deeper and deeper. Through him I realized I had been running from my life. I was running from my pain.

Once I could no longer use running as a way to cope with my life, as a way to escape my life, I knew it was time to have a real "come to Jesus" talk. So I started to pray, and I prayed like never before. I made sure to go to church every Sunday, even in my wheelchair (I have to stop and thank my girlfriends who would take me, one was not a believer, one had to drive a distance to pick me up, but God used both of them to show me love).

TURBULENCE: TRUSTING IN GOD

*"The LORD who rescued me from the paw of the lion
and the paw of the bear will rescue me from the hand of
this Philistine. Saul said to David, go and the LORD be
with you."*
I Samuel 17: 37

I can honestly say, trusting in God the way David did, is
remarkable, and if I were in the same situation, I wonder
if I would have had trusted God to rescue me. So many
times in my life I have not trusted God, but not David. He knew
his God would save him, because he was able to remember how
God had saved him in the past. Therefore, he was able to put
trust in God based on what God had done for him in the past. We
can trust God simply based on God sending his son to die for us,
even when we were God's enemy He loved us so much he sent
his son to die for our sins. But wait there is more, God has
reached down and saved us from bad choices, negative
circumstance, and sin repeatedly.

God uses circumstance/situation to reveal himself to us, and
His plan for our lives. I needed to learn to trust in God, but how?
Where to start?

Let's start with this promise from God:

*"Cast your cares on the Lord and he will sustain you; he will
never let the righteous be shaken." Psalms 55:22*

To cast our cares on Him is to trust Him. Trust He will not leave us, lie to us, or lead us astray. In Hebrew trust means to be secure, confident, or rely on absolutely. Trusting God means to be secure in Him. To be confident He will provide a way when we can't see a way, and to rely on Him and only Him to meet our needs, to sustain us, to love us.

Asking God to take fear and doubt may sound easy, but we make it hard for Him. When we ask God to take something from us, we must be ready to let go.

God will not yank anything from us; we must willingly release it to Him. Then and only then, will God do His part. We have to do our part first, we have to let go. Through letting go we are placing our trust in God, this is what God is waiting for. He is waiting for us to trust him.

"People of Zion, who live in Jerusalem, you will weep no more. How gracious he will be when you cry for help! As soon as he ears, he will answer." Isaiah 30:19

How amazing it this promise from God, when we cry to him, He will hear us and He will answer! What an awesome God we serve.

Think for a minute how dramatically different our lives would be if we trusted God to answer when we cry out to Him. How many times have we made a decision without trusting in God, without even including Him or considering Him in our process?

We serve a God who wants, yes, *wants* to be part of our lives. He wants is to cry out to Him. He is waiting for us to trust with all areas of our lives, not just the easy ones, but all areas.

"Trust in the Lord with all your heart and lean not on your own understanding; in all your ways submit to him and he will make your paths straight." Proverbs 3:5

Right now I want us all to go get some paper, yep, get up, go get paper and pencil (or pen), move....God is waiting.

Now let's write down our fears, and then ceremonially burn them, one at a time, praying over each one, giving each one to

God. Trusting in God to take our fear, our doubt, our hurts, and our loneliness. Burning signifies sacrifice and letting go, and placing all our trust in God to take these things from us in such a manner where we can't pick them back up. Because they are burned and forever given to God.

TURBULENCE: STORMS

"Therefore, if anyone is in Christ, the new creation has come, the old has gone away, and the new is here!"
2 Corinthians 5:17

I think most of the time when flying the turbulence is caused by a storm. The wind, rain, snow, ice, all of these weather related situations can cause us to have a bumpy ride. Some weather issues have actually caused the plane to even crash.

I don't like flying when there is a storm. It's scary and makes my tummy feel icky. However, I live in Colorado so this means most of the time I will experience a storm either on take-off or landing. In these moments I try to pray, this does help to bring me peace, but what happens when the storms of life hit us, usually by surprise?

In this life we will experience many storms. Some are category one hurricanes, some are slow and steady rain fall, and others are wind storms. During the storms it helps to know that, not only is God with me, He is using the storm to for my good.

God uses each storm to clear away old debris making it possible for new growth. Experiencing the storm is scary, it may hurt, and usually is hard. However, when we trust God to use the storm for our good, and when we put our faith and hope in Him, we can see a new future.

Once the storm has passed and the old debris has been removed, we can begin to feel the 'Son", the light of God shinning on us, willing us to grow. Let the storm come and remove the old debris which is holding us back and embrace the light after the storm willing us to grow.

If our focus is on God we can ask "How" instead of "Why". So often when storms hit, we ask God why this is happening instead of asking how I can serve you Lord through this storm?

Storms can come in many different ways, maybe we lose a friend or loved one, or maybe we lose our job, or divorce. One of the most damaging storms is that of betrayal.

Betrayal either by a family member or friend can be devastating. Betrayal leaves us lost, and confused wondering what went wrong, and how we can ever trust again.

The story of Joseph tells us of betrayal and forgiveness. Joseph was the most loved son of Jacob. One day Jacob presented Joseph with a robe made of many colors, symbolizing Jacob's favor for Joseph. However, the other brothers became very jealous of Joseph and Jacob's love for him. The other brothers devised plan to get rid of Joseph, but they decided to not kill him, so they threw him in a pit, and ultimately sold him off for twenty pieces of silver. The Ishmaelite's took Joseph to Egypt. The ten brothers then took Josephs coat to their father, wanting Jacob to believe a wild beast had killed Joseph.

The Ishmaelite's sold Joseph as a slave to Potiphar who worked in King Pharaoh's army. Joseph would not do wrong to please Pharaoh's wife, was wrongly charged with a crime, and sent to prison. But Joseph did not lose his faith, he still held fast to God and God's promise.

Soon, Joseph was put in charge of prisoners, where he met two men, the butler and baker. Joseph began to interpret their dreams, eventually being taken to Pharaoh to interpret his dreams. Joseph acknowledged the power to interpret was not his, but God's. Joseph told him his dreams were the same and Pharaoh made Joseph in charge, giving him his signet ring.

It came to pass Joseph was in charge of giving out of grain. One day Joseph's ten brothers came to buy food and they did not recognize Joseph, but Joseph knew them. They bowed before Joseph, just as Joseph had dreamed years before. Joseph first put them in prison but then his heart was touched, because he could see his brothers were really sorry for the wrong they had done to him. He let them go.

In the end Joseph revealed himself to his brothers and he wept. His brothers brought their father to Joseph. Although Joseph was betrayed by his brothers, Joseph was able with God to forgive them and restore a relationship among them all.

Betrayal is hard. We are hurt, let down, and lost. As with Joseph, God takes these messes and creates something beautiful.

Weathering the storms of life is difficult and often scary, but with God as our pilot we can navigate the stormy waters together.

Our focus on God will bring us through the storms of life daily, must be on him and his will for our lives. Each day God asks us to draw near to Him. God wants to talk to us; He wants to talk with us. He needs to be first in our life, every day. I know for some this may be hard. Let's be honest, we have kids, husbands, jobs, shopping, cleaning, cooking, and the list can go on and on. Remember, all these daily "tasks" should come after our time with God. Even a simple Good Morning God is a great way to start our day. Don't wait until there is time for God. We must make time for God, first thing, not last or when it is convenient or after everyone else has sucked us dry.

Putting God first will change our lives! Give it a try; what do you have to lose? *"God so loved the world he gave his son, that whoever believed would have eternal life." John 3:16.* Don't we owe it to give God our first, our best, every day?

Our daily lives will thrive once we learn to put God first. God will order our steps. Allowing God to speak into our life each day will provide the directional lighting. Pointing us to the appropriate exit sign, taking each of us in the direction he has determined for our life in order to "exit the plane" safely. God does not want us to panic. We need His constant guidance and direction in our lives to know when to move, what to do and how to do it. He wants us to trust in Him, not panic. He wants us to help others along the way, and be patient.

Through the storms and restoration after the storm, our focus should always be on God, for we can do all things through Christ who strengthens us. This verse in Philippians is about know whether we are in a storm or in peace, God is our strength and we are capable of doing anything with Him.

Questions and Points to Ponder

1) What lies from Satan have caused you to make a decision based on fear?

2) How can you take the first step to change from making decision based in fear to making decisions grounded in God's perfect love?

3) What event brought about change for you?

    a.   What moved you from pew sitter to actively engaging in a relationship with God?

4) What do you use to self-medicate, and what are your triggers?

5) How can you let-go and begin to move away from self-medicating to meditating with God?

6) What are of your life are you now trusting God with, and why?

7) What storms has God used to shape you?

8) How can you serve God when the storms come?

CHAPTER FIVE

EXIT ROW: FORGIVENESS

"Love is patient, love is kind, love does not envy or boast; It is not arrogant or rude. It does not insist on its own way, it is not irritable or resentful; it does not rejoice at wrongdoing but rejoices with the truth. "
1 Corinthians 13:4-6

To sit in the exit row, there are qualifying requirements, everyone must be able to assist others, open the exit door, and not panic. In life there are challenges, trials, turbulence, and just plain icky situations, causing us to want to simply to exit, get off the plane and start new, we want to escape. So how can we exit and start new? God is the answer, he gives us the ability to be born again into his family. He gives us new life, eternal life found only in him.

We have all been given the gift of eternal life, once we have accepted Jesus as our Lord and Savior, we are made new.

"For God so loved the world, he gave his only begotten son. That whoever believes in him shall have eternal life" John 3:16

We all know this verse, probably one of the first verses we ever memorized, but today let's digest what it means. God, creator of all things loves the world and all things in the world, so much he sent his son, his son ladies, and can you imagine sending your son to die for mankind? He sent his son to save us sinners. All, yes ALL, those who believe in him will have eternal life. We will have a life outside of this world with the one true God. We have been given the greatest gift--eternal life!

Our life with God starts with forgiveness; he forgives us of our sins, and calls us to forgive those who trespass against us. Remember forgiveness releases us from bondage, anger, and bitterness, it does not mean we have to forget what happened. Although God doesn't remember, as humans we do, this is why it is so very important to ask God to help us to forgive.

To start we need to forgive ourselves, yes, forgive yourself! We are made in God's image, but we are far from perfect. Forgive yourself for not being Betty Crocker and cooking a full meal every night for your family. Forgive yourself for making bad choices and decisions, we all make them. It is time we start letting ourselves off the hook for every bad choice we ever made. Forgive yourself for choosing abortion over life, forgive yourself for drinking too much and ending up with a stranger in your bed. Forgive yourself for looking to things in the world to fill your empty places. God has forgiven you; it is now time for you to forgive yourself. Until we can acknowledge our past mistakes and forgive ourselves, we will not be able to move forward. We are letting our past mistakes drive our future. Unforgiveness will lead to anger. Without forgiveness, anger will fester and grow until it consumes our life.

Anger is another one of Satan's tools to keep us from God's will and loving others. For the most part anger is simply a feeling caused when we experience a failed expectation. Allowed to fester, anger will turn ugly and will eventually destroy the goodness God put inside each of us.

"Get rid of all bitterness, rage, and anger, brawling and slander, along with every form of malice. Be kind and compassionate to one another, forgiving each other as God forgave you." Ephesians 4:31 and 32

A good rule to start living with is simple, not easy, but simple; assume positive intent. When we get upset and want to lash out due to a failed expectation, instead learn to look at the situation/person by assuming positive intent, not malice or evil. Not everyone is "out to get us". As a matter of fact, most people are not, it is our internal judgement based on our own views which leads us to assume the worst intentions from others. Instead learn to assume positive intent, and see how the world will change. We can't let anger and unforgiveness rule our world, we must choose to forgive ourselves, others, and allow God to forgive us. In doing this we are set free.

The woman who simply touched the robe of Jesus was released from her "blood" sickness because of her faith in Jesus. She knew Jesus could forgive her, releasing her of her disease. Jesus will do the same for us, all we must do is believe he is the Son of man, ask him into our hearts, and he will begin his work in us.

Forgiveness sounds easy, but we need God to help us. True forgiveness of ourselves and others means never talking about the hurt again. The hurt and pain might dwell for a bit, but when we truly forgive and ask God to help, we will heal. Forgiveness releases us and gives us new life, resting in the peace of God.

EXIT ROW: GOD'S TIMING

"The LORD said to Samuel, How long will you mourn for Saul, since I have rejected him as king over Israel? Fill your horn with oil and be on your way; I am sending you to Jesse of Bethlehem. I have Chosen one of his sons to be king."
I Samuel 16:1

"So he sent for him and had him brought in. He was glowing with health and had a fine appearance and handsome features. The LORD Said, Rise and anoint him; this is the one. "
1 Samuel 16:12

God will order our steps, in His timing, not ours. I know, I know, in this day of "instant everything" from instant information to instant food, we want what we want right now. Listen ladies, I am here to tell you God doesn't work like the world. His timing is perfect, never early, never late, and always right on time. God wants us to learn patience; He wants us to learn to trust in Him. While we are patiently waiting for that new job, new house, new car, a baby, a husband, healing we need to trust God's timing. It is time for us to lean into God. To pray, to serve, and to love God where we are, and for what He has already given us, eternal life. Trust springs forth patience, and patience produces perseverance. God is not holding out on us, He is holding us back for His perfect timing.

God set us apart, God gave us purpose, each of us has a gift. God wants us to use these gifts to serve Him, and others. He commands us to wait patiently and serve. It is during this time that He is molding us; strengthening us, turning us to fine gold.

"These trials will show that your faith is genuine. It is being tested as fire tests and purifies gold; though your faith is far more precious than mere gold. So when your faith remains strong through many trials, it will bring you much praise and glory and honor on the day when Jesus Christ is revealed to the world." I Peter 1:7

When turbulence in life comes our way, and it will come, we need to trust in God. We need to stop asking "why did this happen?" and start asking "how can I serve God through this circumstance?". Serving God in and through our circumstance will take the focus off our situation, off ourselves and put focus on God, where it belongs. Serving God and others while in a rough spot in our lives gives us purpose, helps us to see a greater picture, and when we serve, we are blessed.

"Whoever serves me must follow me; where I am my servant will be. My father will honor the one who serves me. John 12:26

Divorce is ugly, it is hard, and it hurts. I stated earlier that I have been married twice, neither time was to the man God has for me. So here I sit, 49 years old and divorced. I will be honest; it is hard to wait, to be patient, to listen to God, to be obedient. I get lonely, just like everyone, and in those times of loneliness, I cling to God, for He alone is my comfort, my hope, and my peace.

In this quiet period in my life, I am learning to trust in God, to be patient, to focus my daily life on him, and to serve. I am waiting for my future husband. I have prayed and prayed, and I am still waiting. This is not easy, but it is simple, God will bring my future husband to me, however, it is up to me to keep moving, keep serving, and keep doing what He asks of me until He answers my prayer.

"So the man gave names to all the livestock, the birds in the sky and the wild animals. But for Adam no suitable helper was found. So the Lord God caused the man to fall into a deep sleep; and while he was sleeping, he took one of the man's ribs and then closed up the flesh. Then the Lord God made a woman from the rib he had taken out of the man, and brought her to the man". Genesis 2:20-22

I live each day knowing, trusting in this promise from God, He will bring me to my future husband. I don't need to help God find my mate, God already knows who he is and in His timing, He will bring me to my future husband.

God will do the same for each of us. In His timing He will bring about the new job, husband, baby, house, and healing. Trust in Him.

Goliath

I am brought to the story of David. I am sure many of us are familiar with the "big" stories of David. David and Goliath, David and Bathsheba, but what about the true story of David? The story of his faith, patience, and prayer life before acting.

David was the youngest son of Jesse, and he was a worrier. He had a heart for God and God knew David would always follow Him. David did conquer Goliath and he did obsess over Bathsheba, ultimately killing her husband. Oh, but there is a deeper story, David waited, truly waited for God.

David was young (not sure exact age) when God had Samuel anoint him to be king, but then it took somewhere around ten years (theologians don't have an exact amount of time) for him to become king. He was thirty when he became king, but he waited for a very long time for this to happen.

Two things strike me about David, one, was his ability to wait, to be patient, never losing faith, even though year after year went by and nothing seemed to be happening. Second, David always inquired with God before "moving", especially before going into battle. God always answered.

David never asked God, when am I going to be king, he only asked God for provision, guidance, and deliverance. God was always faith to answer.

What this says to me is, no matter how long we wait, ten minutes, ten months, or ten years, God is with us. When we need to know what to do next, ask, God will provide an answer. He will guide us. Until finally the day will come, God's perfect plan, in His perfect timing will be complete and we will get that job, move to that beautiful house, find out we are pregnant, get married, and so on.

David had faith. He knew God would always answer when he called. I challenge everyone out there to trust God, have faith in God like David. Never losing sight of where God is taking us, even if it takes longer than we would like.

There is a way for us to exit the plane and start anew, it is up to us to believe in God, forgive ourselves, forgive others and allow Him to forgive us. We must learn to give our best to God, give him our firsts each and every day! We must focus on him and his plan for our lives by trusting in Him, in His timing, and letting Him direct our path.

Have faith, God is not done with us. He is making us strong and courageous for our next phase.

Questions and Points to Ponder

1) What do you need to forgive yourself for?

2) What do you need to forgive someone else of?

    a. The act of forgiveness doesn't mean we continue to be hurt, it simply sets us free from the control, from the pain.

3) What are you trusting God to provide in His timing?

    a. How can you lean into God in this time?

    b. How is God providing during a period of waiting?

4) What is your greatest hope?

CHAPTER SIX

SMOOTH LANDING: BUILDING A RELATIONSHIP WITH GOD

"In this is love, not that we loved God, but that HE loved us."
1 John 4:10

Relationships are hard, husband/wife, sibling, parent/child, bestie, and even co-worker. So how can we have a relationship with our God? He is so mighty, so great, and so powerful, how can we ever feel worthy of such a relationship? Well, to be perfectly frank, nothing we could ever do, or not do, will create an environment for a relationship with God; this relationship is solely dependent upon our willingness.

Unlike our other "earthly" relationships, God calls to us, He is waiting for us, and is always ready to build a relationship with us, it is all of us who struggle to reach out to God. Some may not reach out due to fear, some because of shame, and some simply because we often don't know how to even start. Some might wonder why we need a relationship, I mean, doesn't God love us unconditionally anyway?

Let's take a look at what God says about having a relationship with Him.

"Jesus said to them, I am the way, and the truth, and the life. No one comes to the Father except through me." John 14:6

Here we see Jesus himself telling us the only way to God is through Him. What does this mean?

It means Jesus came to provide the way to God. Prior to Jesus, no Gentile or "everyday" Jewish person could approach the temple of God, but through Jesus' life, death, and resurrection. Everyone now has access to God. God wants to have a relationship with all of His people, He wants a relationship so bad He sent his only son to earth, to become human, to die for us and to rise again.

Wow! Let that sink in. God's desire for a relationship meant giving us His only son. He created us to have a relationship with Him (if we choose).

How? That is the question. We understand the why, now we need to understand the how? How do we have a relationship with the highest God?

Well, it is "simple" as any other relationship, by spending time together. I know it sounds too easy, but it is the truth. All we have to do is spend time with God and the relationship will build and grow. Like other relationships, when you don't spend time with God you will notice you miss Him.

Spend time with God daily, in prayer, in worship, in conversation. God is ready, it is now up to us.

We have all been granted the unique luxury of spending time with God each day. It is up to us to choose spending time with God over the many other distractions in life.

Part of this relationship with God involves a prayer life. To do this we need to put God first. Pray in the morning, before we start our day, before life kicks in. Before you know it, it's dinner time, the kids are needing help with homework, and your husband is trying to tell you about his day. Then there is cooking to be done, and then we fall into bed at 9:30 after doing the dishes and laundry, and making lunches for the next day, exhausted. All we can muster is a brief acknowledgement to God for the day before we fall asleep while trying to pray.

Give God your first, your best, not your leftovers.

"But seek the kingdom of God and his righteousness, and all these things shall be added to you." Matthew 6:33

Seek God first, seek God throughout your day. Most of all let God speak to you. Most often when we pray, we spend so much time making requests of God we don't allow God to speak and direct us. How can he direct our life if we don't allow Him time to speak and tell us the path He has for us?

Once God has spoken, let His words be all you need to hear, don't add to it. Don't try to interpret meaning, don't overthink, simply let God's words be God's words. God is not a God of confusion, He will give clear instruction when the time comes, so we don't need to try and figure out the meaning of His words. If God tells you "it is time" don't try to determine what He is talking about. He will let you know, believe me, I have learned this the hard way.

Too many times I have taken God's words and tried to force them into an answer to prayer, trying to make my future happen. One day I was in my bathroom, getting ready for my day and I heard "just friends". Now ladies this was a very clear answer to a prayer about a man in my life. However, because I wanted what I wanted, I turned these words into what I wanted, meaning instead of this being exactly what it meant "just friends". I turned it into, it must mean we are just friends now and will build to more later, again forcing a relationship which was not from God. You know, making sure I was in control of my future (by the way, I would not recommend doing things how I did, it is very backwards and incredibly wrong). It was very clear what God meant, I simply chose to see it how I wanted things, instead of simply hearing God's words and letting them be the final answer.

Ladies, when we pray and ask God for answers, we truly need to be ready to accept His answers, and not try to manipulate His words into what we want.

Let his words be His words, for His words are true.

"Yet the Lord longs to be gracious to you; therefore, he will rise up to show you compassion. For the Lord is a God of justice. Blessed are all that wait for him. People of Zion, who live in Jerusalem, you will weep no more. How gracious he will be when you cry for help! As soon as he hears, he will answer you. Although the Lord gives you the bread of adversity and the water of affliction, your teachers will be hidden no more; with your own eyes you will see them. Whether you turn to your right or left, your ears will hear a voice behind you saying "this is the way, walk in it." Isaiah 30: 18-21

These verses are so packed with instruction; I am not sure where to begin. First, the Lord longs to be gracious to us. Wow, this alone is amazing, considering the life I have led. God wants to be gracious to me is so utterly awesome! The Lord will show us compassion and be gracious. How is this possible? God loves us so much, that's how!

God will instruct us, did you read that? At every turn, to our right or left, God will instruct us. We will see and hear his voice telling us which way to go.

This is a promise from God, He will not leave us or forsake us. He will always guide our steps. However, we must choose to be in relationship with Him, we must spend time with Him in prayer. We need to give God time to speak to us, to guide our path. A strong relationship with God is our foundation for every other relationship we will ever experience.

I sit in awe and fear of God as He is the creator of all things. He is my king, my guide, my husband, my father, and my everything. It is my great honor to have a relationship with God.

SMOOTH LANDING: SUBMISSION

"I delight to do you will O God, your law is within my heart."
Psalm 40:8

A m I the only woman on the planet to react with "um, no, I am not submitting to anything or anyone?" The first time I heard "submit" it felt like I would never be able to truly submit to God or any man (maybe this is why my marriages went bad). I was after all "wonder-woman", I need no help, I need no one, and I can do it all, or so says the women's code book. Years ago the word submit would conger up all kinds of unpleasant thoughts and I honestly just wanted to run, run far, far away.

Then one day God started to reveal His meaning of submission to me. I had one of those ah-ha moments, and my thoughts and feeling started to change. I started to change, and the more I changed, the more God clarified what He wants from us and how we should not only submit to Him but to each other!

"Submit to one another, out of reverence for Christ. Wives submit to your husbands as you do the Lord. For the husband is the head of the wife and Christ is the head of the

78

Church, his body of which he is savior, The Church submits to Christ, so also should wives submit to their husbands in everything. "

"However, each one of you also must love his wife as he loves himself, and the wife must respect her husband"
Ephesians 5:21-24 and Ephesians 5:33

The Greek word for submit is "hupotasso" and means to obey or "to arrange in order under". This word submit was originally a military term and was only used twelve times in the Bible (KJV). If we think about it, this would make perfect sense. Each military level must arrange itself below and obey the senior level above. In the same way God is telling us we must arrange ourselves below him and obey him first, then others, putting our needs last.

In reality, submission was/is not the "ugly" word the world wants us to think it was/is, and it did not mean I would lose my opinion or voice, or ability to make decisions, or even my identity. It doesn't mean I am "less than". Quite the opposite, it means there is a natural order, ordained by God, with him seated on the God head throne.

Submission is an act of love, an outward expression of an inward devotion or desire to please God. We will always fall short, but God's grace and love is enough. How can we not submit to Him? How can we tell God, oh I just can't do the submission thing, anything else you want but not submission. God wants all of us, every square inch, everything! If we hold out on submitting to Him, we miss the point of His existence. If we say no to submission, we are saying no to God's plan, God's will and God's desire for our life. We are telling Him we want to be in control. Ladies, this is one of the most important decisions we will ever make. Submission or not, which will you choose?

Submission to God is our key to freedom, not imprisonment.

In this command we are also told to submit to others. This is everyone submitting to everyone, everyone putting the person next to you before our own. Married or not, we are called to submit first to God then to others (including a husband if married). Submission is God's way of letting us all know how much He loves us. By submitting to Him, we are saying to God "your will, not my own".

One point I want to make perfectly clear, many reading this will say, what about if someone is in an abusive relationship (verbal, emotional, physical, sexual, all or a combination) should they have to submit to their husband. Well, this is a bit tricky, so I will say this: God does not want any of us to be someone's scapegoat, doormat, or punching bag, period. Now, that being said, if the situation is dangerous to us, or our kids, or family, please, please get to a safe place. God can and will work miracles in our hearts, minds, and souls, however, we do not need to be subjected to abuse until such time as God makes changes in the other person (inflicting the abuse). I am not saying get divorced (this decision is between you and God).

Submission is about love not abuse and control.

Submission to God is our key to freedom,

not imprisonment

Because,

Submission is about love,

not abuse and control.

SMOOTH LANDING: PURITY

"To the pure, all things are pure. But to those who are corrupted and do not believe, nothing is pure."
Titus 1:15

What does purity mean to each of us? When we talk of purity many jump right to thinking of sexual purity, and the bible does warm us against sexual immorality many times, but I think there is so much more. Sexual purity is only a piece of the purity puzzle. There are many pieces, that when put together will create a beautiful picture of what a pure mind/thoughts, a pure heart/soul, pure physical/sexual life will bring.

"Create in me a pure heart of God, and renew a right steadfast spirit within me.
Psalms 51:10

Our purity begins with our hearts. What is in our heart will drive our thoughts and our actions. How can we have a pure heart with everything we have experienced in this life? This is not easy, yet the answer is simple, we have to choose to allow God to heal our hearts (we will cover this subject more in the next chapter).

Without healing our hearts are scared and open. We are oozing negativity and bitterness. We search and search for something, anything to stop and heal our wounded heart. To stop the bleeding, but we find no amount of drugs or alcohol, number of hours we might spend working, or working out, no level of business, or person can bring us any relief. Maybe there is a temporary relief, but in the end we wake to a new day still bleeding, not fulfilled, and the cycle continues.

We continue on this never-ending hamster wheel, going round and round each day, searching, the endless searching to feel better. We can even get lost on this wheel, lost in the land of numbness, because numbness feels better than hurt and pain. The numbness is better than the never-ending bleeding. So we keep going, numb, but we keep going.

How can we stop the hamster wheel, how can we get off and find something better, more fulfilling? We must turn to God, for with Him, we can be healed. God is the only one who can heal our broken hearts, and that can stop the bleeding forever. God is our answer. God is THE answer.

We must turn to God and allow Him to heal our hearts. In this healing we are made new; we are renewed in God's love, thus, purifying our heart.

This purification of heart does not stop: it is on-going and forever. Once we allow God access to our heart, He will forever be there to renew us, to fill holes caused by hurt, and to fulfill us.

Once our hearts are pure, everything else will follow, and our thoughts will be in alignment to God and will become pure.

In Philippians 4:8 God calls us to think about things which are true, and noble, right, and pure. I know this is not always possible. We are human, so when that lady at the grocery store rushes ahead of you to get to the check-out line right before you, and you only have two items, and she has a full basket, our thoughts might not be pure. However, God is talking about intentionally thinking of good things, noble things, and pure things.

With a pure heart, we must deliberately turn our thoughts from ugliness to pure. This means when bad or negative thoughts enter our mind, we must immediately and intentionally dismiss them. This is especially true when we start listening to Satan's lies and we start having thoughts of doubt and fear.

Our ability to recognize Satan and his lies will give us an advantage in the Spiritual fight for purity. *One of our greatest weapons is discerning God's truth from Satan's lies.* Once we are able, with pure heart and pure thought, to see the lie as a lie, the quicker we can dismiss the lie and remove the doubt and fear from our thoughts. Thus leaving us able to move on with our thoughts and focus on God.

I know we all want to know how to recognize the lie. Well this is a little harder and it takes knowing God, and allowing God to move in our lives to truly know when we hear from Satan and when we hear from God. Knowing God as we read in previous chapters is about having a relationship with Him, spending time with Him, and talking with Him. When we build this relationship with God we will recognize His voice, therefore, making it easier to know and recognize Satan's lies.

Our heart drives our thoughts, which drive our actions.

> *One of our greatest weapons is discerning God's truth from Satan's lies*

Physical purity consists of different pieces too. There is purity in our eyes or what we see, purity in our actions or what we do, and sexual purity. Purity with our eyes starts with what are allowing ourselves to view, see, consume? What kind of movies are we watching or TV shows? What kind of magazines are we perusing?

What our eyes consume, will impact our thoughts

In order to have purity of sight, we need to first declare a covenant with God. A covenant is a contract or pledge, committing to God we will turn from impure TV or movies. We will turn from gazing at the "super hot" man at the gym or beach, we will in turn focus on seeing well.

I know ladies, this is hard, we want to watch that funny TV show that everyone is talking about. We want to watch the romantic love story. Heck we want to look at the really nice looking man. We think, it's just TV, or a movie, or even with the man at the gym or beach we might think, I will never see him again, what is the harm? Well, this is how Satan pulls us in, with the small stuff. Each time we watch that TV show, or watch a movie with sex before marriage, or gaze at the man at the gym, we become less and less sensitive to God and His commandments, this will leave us wide open for Satan to swoop in and devour us.

Take for instance David and Bathsheba. 2 Samuel 11 tells us about how David, who should have gone off to war but instead decided to stay, leaving him in the village when the other men were off to war. This is a lesson in itself about choices. But we will continue. As he was awakened one evening, he saw Bathsheba bathing. Now right here, in this moment, David should have walked away, but his eyes were drawn to her beauty. So, David watched her bathe, and this began a stirring within him. He had to have her, even though he had found out she was married, he still sent for her and slept with her. Then she finds out she is pregnant, how can this ever be explained, for her husband was off at war? The story continues on and we learn he crafts a plan to have her husband return from battle and sleep with his wife. But Uriah was a soldier and felt if his men were at battle he would not enjoy the company of his wife, this was wrong, so he did not sleep with Bathsheba, leaving David in a serious predicament. David ultimately determines to have Uriah killed in battle so he can have Bathsheba and she would not be judged for being pregnant (indicating she committed adultery, which was punishable by death).

Ladies, just one glance, just one look, is a very slippery slope, which can lead to greater and greater sin. This is why we must be in covenant with God to commit to not looking, to not allowing our eyes to consume inappropriate, ungodly images. Looking is harmful because it so often leads to sexual immorality.

I am sure most of us have heard the old adage "Why buy the cow when you can get the milk for free". This is so very true! This world wants us to think it's okay to have sex before your married, especially for those who have been married before. God couldn't possibly be asking people who have had sex with an ex-spouse to now not have sex, right? Well, as a matter of fact, yes, that is exactly what God is telling us. Physical and sexual restraint is not a punishment it is gift. When we restrain from sex we can see, I mean truly see, the other person for who they really are without the confusion caused by feeling manufactured by sleeping together.

When two people have sex they become one, and for most women out there feeling are aroused, causing us to "over feel" for someone too soon. Meaning, our feelings want us to believe we are "in love" but the truth is we are "in lust". Our physical needs and desires override us into believing we love someone, when in fact we don't even know them (I say this because most couples begin a sexual relationship within a few weeks of dating, thus, not giving enough time to get to know each other). When we allow our feeling manufactures from sex interfere with assessment of someone we lose objectivity, thus, losing the ability to see "red flags" or warnings.

Sex before marriage is not allowed, it is not okay and God does see this as a sin.

For many of us, we have already been sexually immoral so how can we become pure? Our quest for purity can start now, it can start immediately. We need to cry out to God for forgiveness, we can make a covenant with Him to remain pure of heart, soul, mind, spirit and body. In His forgiveness we are cleansed, we are pure, now it is up to us to make choices to keep allowing God to heal us when we are hurt, to keep our thoughts pure and our eyes on Him.

What our eyes consume, will impact our thoughts.

SMOOTH LANDING: W.O.R.T.H.

"For God so loved the world, he gave his one and only Son, that whoever believes in him shall not perish but have eternal life. For God did not send his Son into the world to condemn the world, but to save the world through him."
John 3:16

"Actions speak louder than words." 1856, Abraham Lincoln

Unless one has lived in a remote location of the world, I am quite sure, both the verse and the colloquialism are familiar. So familiar, it is easy to simply gloss over the meaning/impact. I want to really dig into what John wants to convey to us in John 3:16. It is a verse many of us have memorized (probably in Sunday school as a young child), so now that we are adults, what does this verse mean and how does it change our life perspective?

Going back to chapter two, we discussed knowing and accepting our identity in Christ. I want to take this idea a bit further to include knowing, accepting, and receiving our worth found only in Christ. Worth is "the level at which someone or something deserves to be valued." Which means we deserve to be valued at Christ's level. Wow, I don't know about all of you, but the idea of being valued at Christ's level is mind blowing!

How is this possible? I   am a sinner, and I daily fall short. How can I deserve to be valued? It is quite simple ladies, we deserve to be valued at Christ's level because God sent His only Son, to die for us, for our sin, and for all our shortcomings. He loved us so much and wanted to restore us, and to have a relationship with us He sent His Son to die for us.

He loved us in action, immediately placing worth upon us.

I have struggled for many, many years to accept and receive worth placed upon me by God. As I have written about in previous chapters, our identity and now worth, is difficult to grasp because we have spent so many years believing what others say about us or comparing ourselves to others, believing and only settling for something or someone "less than" because we don't feel like we are worth something greater. To tell you the truth, this has been the most difficult part of my journey with God. I struggle to this day with my worth, my head always knows, it is my heart which trips me up sometimes. How we can begin to digest, to understand and finally receive our worth? I think for that to happen we must start at the beginning.

We should ask ourselves, what and when have we settled, and why? Write these things down for future reference. Some may have settled on a job, or house, or lifestyle or spouse, there are various "things" which we settle on. For me, it has always been my boyfriend/spouse. I have settled for a couple of reasons, one is I never felt lovable. Remember back in previous chapters I wrote about my dad leaving and other life events? These triggered me to thinking I am not lovable, therefore, making poor choice for a mate. Second, I have never chosen a mate who loved me enough to fight for me, for us, for our relationship. I was always with men who simply left, either on their own or because I broke things off, but never once did any of them fight to keep the relationship. This left me with a rather large, gaping hole in my heart, causing me to continue to search for love in all the wrong places. Settling for someone less than, because I felt less than.

As my walk with God matured and our relationship grew, I was able to see how terribly wrong my thought process was, and how I had let what others thought, felt, and said, mattered more to me than God. I had made choices which hurt me, time and time again, and was not able to change the cycle until I really started to grasp my worth placed upon me by God.

> *He loved us in action, immediately placing worth upon us.*

Part of maturing in my relationship with God was realizing I needed help. He was the only one who could really help me. No counselor alive today can heal the way God can. Counselors can help, but know it is God who does the changing.

I started with a list of things I needed God to heal, and I prayed over them, giving them to God and asking God heal the holes created in my heart caused by each one. Every hurt, betrayal, and disillusionment in life, every failed expectation, and failed relationship I gave to God. In giving these to God I realized, as human beings God does not expect us to not have feelings, quite the opposite. However, He does not want us to set-up camp in the midst of our feelings and live there. We need to understand we will have feelings (anger, bitterness, jealousy, envy, hurt, sadness, etc.), and we need to allow ourselves to "feel" each and every one, then let then go, and cry out to our loving God asking for healing. God will hear us, He will heal us (sometimes not in the way we think or want, but He will always heal). *Let God's "love putty" fill the holes in our heart caused by the hurts of this world.* As His love fills in our holes, we will heal and before you know it, we will be seeing ourselves as God sees us-- worthy of the love he has placed on us.

I was teaching a single women's class on waiting for God to bring you your spouse. One night we were all sitting on my back porch, the sun was setting, and one of the women said "You know, we are worthy, we are beautiful, and we are the Prime Rib." This stuck with me because it is so simple, yet so far from what we believe to be true. Ladies, we are the Prime Rib of Adams rib, God formed us from Adam, and we became the best of the best, the Prime Rib!

Before we were born God knew us, He created us, and He loved us so much he sent His son, in human form, to live on earth, to suffer, to die and raise again. For us! That my friend truly depicts "actions speaking louder than words".

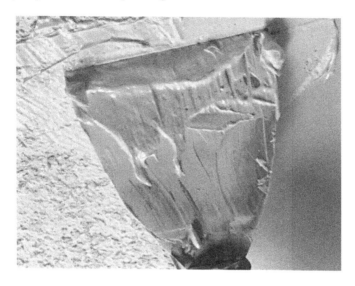

I now see my worth is not found in my weight, my clothing size, how many miles I can run, my job, my kids, or a spouse, rather it was placed upon me through Jesus' death and resurrection. My worth, your worth, was freely given to us, it is now our choice to accept and receive it.

How will our lives change by simply receiving worth which God has placed upon us? Would we make different choices, would we love deeper, would we live with joy and peace? Let's ask God right now.

Father God, you are a gracious God, a merciful God and a loving God. Please take away our pain by filling in our hurts with your love, please allow us to accept and receive the worth you have placed upon us, in Jesus name, Amen!

> *Let God's "love putty" fill the holes in our heart caused by the hurts of this world.*

Questions and Points to Ponder

1) How are you building a deeper, stronger relationship with God?

     a. This task can be daunting, so start small, start with simply saying good morning God (before getting out of bed) and good night God (before drifting off to sleep).

2) What is your greatest fear about submission?

     a. How can your new, stronger relationship with God help to overcome this fear?

3) What area of purity do you struggle with and how can focusing on your relationships with God impact/change your struggle into an achievement?

4) What or who caused you to feel unworthy?

5) What holes do you need God to cover with His "love putty"?

CHAPTER SEVEN

WAITING .... ENDLESS WAITING

"However, no one knows the day or hour when these things will happen, not even the angels in heaven or the Son himself. Only the Father knows."
Matthew 24:36

The day was here, I had been paying for this vacation for a year, saving money for "extras". The anticipation had built, and now they day had arrived. All I wanted was to get to my destination, but in front of me were 20 long, grueling hours. So, began the waiting. First waiting at the initial airport, then the flight to Texas (where the others would join me the following day to continue the journey to Jamaica), but for now it was just me and my son. We arrived in Texas at about 10 PM, sigh, still ten hours until the others arrived. What does one do in an airport for ten hours, at night? NOTHING. There is absolutely nothing to do, we were lucky to find a "quiet" spot near our departure gate to try and rest (which is nearly impossible due to frigid cold). I tried sleeping first, one of us tried to stay awake (for safety purposes), but like I said it was FREEZING. I don't mean a little. I think the airport purposely turns up the air conditioning to keep people from sleeping in the airport. It was so uncomfortable, even with a blanket. I think I finally nodded off about midnight, and slept for a couple hours, then my son needed to sleep, so I woke up and let him rest for bit. At the end he only slept about two hours, so now it is only four am. We still had five hours, oh the time was DRAGGNG on. All I wanted was a very large coffee, that didn't open until five thirty. So I began counting down the minutes until I could walk over and get a cup. Tic-Tock, tick-tock, the minutes slowly crept by, until finally, yes, I could get a coffee. Can I say, that was one of the best cups of coffee I have ever had! I enjoyed every single drop. Then it was back to our departure gate for more, waiting. We tried to make small talk (which by now was difficult as we were both very tired and over the waiting). The sun was coming up, this gave us hope, only a little while now. Tic-Tock, minutes crawled by. Then I receive "the" text, they had landed and were on their way to the gate, again, minutes ticking by so slowing. Where were they? It was taking forever! Then, around the corner, I see the pack coming and can hardly wait, so I begin to move towards them to shrink the space between us, and hugs abounded for a few minutes. I was so very glad to see them, because with their arrival, it meant we were about to board and continue our journey to our Jamaica get away. Upon arriving in Jamaica, hours (20 total) of waiting, slipped away and were a distant memory because the waiting had ended, and I had made it to the destination.

Have you ever waited on something or someone and it seems the minutes, hours, days, months, years are ticking by so slowly, the anticipation is so great you can hardly contain yourself? My example is one of many thousand examples of waiting. Waiting is hard, it can be frustrating, it can be overwhelming, but in the waiting, we can embrace peace, joy, and love. Because our hope for what we wait for is found in God. It is in the waiting we can learn patience and perseverance.

I have imagined what life would be like if we didn't have to wait (not too much imagination required, our world is already an "instant" gratification society) and it is a scary thought. Think of driving, we must wait for traffic signals. Not to irritate us but for our safety and safety of others. If there were no traffic signals, just think of the chaos and the loss of life. Or how about waiting to have intimate relations until married? I can say this didn't happen in my life (as you have all read, this led to heartache and disappointment).

When God asks us to wait, He is not punishing us. He is preparing us for what is coming next, and because we can't see the future, how can we possibly prepare without waiting? Waiting can seem endless, but it is not, for God has given us a promise. His timing is always perfect, always right on time, never late.

"There is a time for everything, and a season for every activity under the heavens."
Ecclesiastes 3:1

Let's talk about waiting, and feeling ashamed at the same time. Noah waited, first for the flood, then during the flood, and finally after the flood. If we rushed into everything without preparation, what good would come of it? *Once we can embrace the significant moments in the waiting, we can experience the joy in the waiting.* Without the waiting, there is no anticipation, no expectation of what is to come, leaving the world dull and uninterested. Because we have not had to wait and work towards the things we want, instead they have simply given to us leaving us feeling empty and constantly wanting more and more to fill the emptiness.

As Christian women we are all waiting, waiting for Jesus to return, and how wonderful that day will be? The anticipation of Christ's return is unbelievably awesome, and something we all WANT to wait for, something we are all WILLING to wait for because we can be excited about meeting Jesus and all the others in heaven. It is this type of anticipation we should seek in all circumstance which God calls us to wait. No matter if you are sitting today, waiting for that new job, or for your husband to return to you, or for that baby you long for, or for your loved one to be drug free, or "you fill in the blank", *everything worthwhile is worth the waiting in between.*

I am not saying it is easy. I am not saying you will love every second. I am saying when we are able to seek God in the waiting. We can understand it's in the waiting God prepares us, we can find peace, we can find joy. We can find hope because we are placing our trust in God to fulfill His promise, and not in the world.

While I was sitting in the airport, I was able to persevere because I KNEW where I was going. Life is usually not that simple. We usually are waiting for unknown amounts of time, for an unknown ending, this part my friends is hard.

I am in a period of waiting, I am waiting for my future husband (yes ladies, I do long to be married, again, for the last time). I have been waiting for over a year, and during that time I have drawn closer to God. I have found things out about me (some I like and will keep, some I don't like and I am changing). There are days when I WISH I had someone with me to climb the mountains of life. Then I realize, God is with me and He is strengthening me and preparing me for whatever comes next. I have learned to be joyous in my circumstance and to focus on where God is taking me instead of focusing on where I have been. Some days are hard, and I will be honest, I do not understand why God can't just bring this wonderful man He has for me to me right now! Then God asked me to sign up for two on-line dating sites, so I did, and right away there were two men. Each taught me something, one reminded me to pay attention to actions, not words (something God put on my heart two years ago, I used to pay more mind to words than actions). The other reminded me I am a daughter of the King and thus, will not compromise my sexual purity for anyone. Neither worked out (in terms of dating) but God used both to reinforce lessons he wants me to remember. It is easy to not have sex when you are not dating, but God is preparing me for the "real deal" by strengthening my resolve through these "practice" runs.

Today each of us are struggling with waiting, maybe your biological clock is ticking, and you may think time is running out, remember Sarah and Abraham. Maybe, like me, you are aging and you think your beauty is fading. Who will want this old, dried up woman? Remember Boaz and Ruth. Maybe you are waiting on a better job, or a new house, remember the birds who never worry about food or lodging for God provides for them each day. Maybe you are waiting for an illness to be taken away, or an addition removed, remember God is preparing each one of us for our future (we have no idea how God will use the illness or addiction for His glory, but He will).

Ladies, it is not easy waiting on Gods timing, but I know when God's plan for our lives is revealed. Oooooohhhhh it will be worth the waiting! Have hope my friends, God is with us always, even in the tears, in the endless hours, days, months, years of waiting, He is there, preparing us for our future.

> *Once we can embrace the significant moments in the waiting, we can experience the joy in the waiting.*

Questions and Points to Ponder

1) What have you been asking God for? What are you waiting on?

a. How can you find peace and joy in the waiting?

b. How is God preparing you in the time of waiting?

2) What has God called you to do in your period of waiting?

a. God doesn't want us to sit around and focus on what might be, He wants us to be actively working in His kingdom.

CHAPTER EIGHT

LANDING GEAR: COMMUNITY

"For as in one body we have many members and the members do not all have the same function, so we, though many, are one body in Christ, and individually members one of another."
Romans 12: 4-5

In case of change in cabin pressure, an oxygen mask will deploy. Please be sure to secure your mask before helping others. Hmm, two things strike me about this. One is, we all need oxygen to live. In as much as God is our oxygen. Second, these instructions should be extremely familiar to anyone who travels by air. However, I can see clearly in my life where I haven't followed these very simple instructions. How can we help someone else if we have not securely fastened God as our oxygen mask to everything we do? Our every breath is from God, therefore, we can't proceed in our lives without Him as the air we breathe. Subsequently, we are not equipped to help others until we have oxygen flowing through us. It all starts with us taking action to allow God to be our air, allowing God to sustain us. This will enable us and give us power to help others.

Remember back in the day, when we were young? Going to the playground was so much fun! I loved the swings, it always felt so freeing, wind in my face, floating in the open air. I just loved it. Sometimes when the swings were full (which I learned to live with, but didn't like) I was forced, yes forced, to pick something else to do during recess. I also liked the teeter-totter, but this requires two people for it to work. Here was my biggest dilemma, who would I ask to join me? I know you may find this hard to believe, but in elementary school I was kind of the quiet kid, more to myself, so picking someone to join me on the teeter-totter was a big deal. I was also the "ugly duckling", so I was not with the popular crowd. This really limited my options for a teeter-totter partner. Eventually I would find someone, usually they were sitting alone or doing something else alone and I would ask, they would usually join me and we would enjoy the ride on the teeter-totter.

In our Christian walk, we need a teeter-totter partner, someone to ride the up's and down's with us, to help push us up when we are down and to help keep us grounded when we are up. God is so wonderful, He sends us just the right people at just the right time to be our partners, this is also called our community (or as I like to call it "my tribe").

Our community or tribe are the people God puts into our lives to anchor us, to pray for us, and with us as we all navigate this world. My tribe is full of wonderfully unique and beautiful ladies who come from different walks, and who all play a specific role in my life. I need them as much as they need me. I know who to go to with each specific trial or test/challenge. It is important to stay connected to each woman in my tribe. I mean really connected, not just during group ladies night out activities, but outside of those special nights, the one on one coffee or lunch dates. This is where the relationship blossoms and true connections are made and cultivated. I know this takes time, effort, and energy, which we don't always feel like using, but I am here to tell you, make the effort. Use your energy, take the time to cultivate these relationships, because when faced with devastating loss or extreme excitement, your tribe will be there with you supporting and encouraging you every step of the way. We need each other, God designed us humans to need one another, so take that chance, be brave, reach out to that friend, connect, cultivate, and be in community.

> *In our Christian walk, we need a teeter-totter partner, someone to ride the up's and down's with us, to help push us up when we are down and to help keep us grounded when we are up.*

Another important piece in our community or tribe is our church, and within the church, life groups or Bible study groups. I can remember when I first started going to my church and they were talking about life groups. I was like, what is a life group and why do we need to be in one? Well that was ten years ago and I am so very thankful for life groups. I have learned some of the most important relationships in my life originate within the life group. I tried two before landing in the one which changed my life. This first two were more about me understanding what life group was all about, and learning to commit to going, no matter what. Then, oh then I joined "the group", the one which helped change me, to transform me into a person who looked forward to going to life group and eventually the woman called to lead women's life groups.

The group I joined which was "the group" was filled with different folks, mostly families, but we were all so very different. We were in different places in our journey with God, but we all simply "clicked", right from the start. In this group I learned to share my faith, share my story (testimony), and to be vulnerable. In my vulnerability, God created the greatest of friendships, one with a woman much younger than I, one with a woman who was much further along in her Spiritual maturity than I, one who was a great listener, one who would help me to regain range of motion in my legs, one who was a daughter from within the group, one who would introduce me to the book "Choosing God's Best". We all connected, through similar, and not so similar, life stories. God put us all together, for two years, and it was magical! I mean really magical, each life group brought us closer together. Through God, good food, and laughter we all became fast friends. This group disbanded after two years. I started my own woman's life group, others started their own groups, but I will forever be thankful for the two years I had with all of them! It was sad to leave, but I knew it was time. God had used this group to prepare me for what was ahead, my own group, my ministry, and even this book.

Church is important, I know not everyone believes this to be true, but I do. Sunday mornings are for being with God, in Church, with others, who, like me, believe in God. We come together to worship Him to be in His presence as a community, as one body, praising Him, and giving Him glory. This is where we can be exposed to Life groups, volunteer opportunities within our Church or community. During the week we have personal time with God, but on Sunday (or for some, Saturday), we have community time with God, as He designed. It is so important for us to come together, Jesus showed us how to do it, He came together with His disciples often.

Friends are wonderful, especially when life is not so great. How about that one friend (or more) who will always tell the truth, say it like it is, even when she knows it will hurt? We all need some of these friends, because they are the ones who hold us accountable for walking the Christian walk, for pushing us out of our comfort zone spiritually to allow for greater, deeper relationship with God and others.

God has called us to love one another, in this, the greatest of all commandments. In actively, intentionally, living this out, everyday, we will impact others lives for Christ. We are His hands and His feet, *we are the very essence of Gods love, manifest in human form. God uses us to present Himself to the world.* Be brave, reach out, open your heart, your home, your spirit to allow you to love the way God loves. We were not made to live this life in a "Christian" bubble, no ladies, we were made to glorify God in all we do, every single day.

We are the very essence of God's love, manifest in human form. God uses us to present Himself to the world.

Questions and things to Ponder

1) Where has God called you to serve in His body?

2) By telling God's story of your life, who could benefit?

3) Who is your teeter-totter partner? Why?

4) How does being involved with Church fulfill God's command?

5) If you are not involved at Church, what is one small step you can take to being engaging?

CHAPTER NINE

ARRIVAL: PLANS

"For the word of God is living and active, sharper than any two-edged sword, piercing to the division of soul and spirit, of joints and of marrow, and discerning the thoughts and intentions of the heart."
Hebrews 4:12

The most anticipated event for most trips is arriving at the destination. Once we land, we can begin to let the world go, and enjoy the time ahead to focus on rest, relationships, and fun, or simply enjoy arriving back home. Think back to a trip, either when youngster or older, and think about the anticipation. The "are we there yet" mentality. I can almost feel it, bubbling up inside. Oh the fun to be had! But what happens to the anticipation, the excitement if the flight is delayed, diverted, or worse cancelled? If the trip suddenly requires a change in plans? I remember, once I was on a business trip, and on my way home the flight was diverted to another airport, due to heavy hail and rain. Wow, the anticipation of being in my home, in my bed disappeared in an instant.

I don't know about you ladies, but I live to plan. For me half of the fun in the trip is in the planning, which creates anticipation and excitement. I like to create spreadsheets (my girlfriends give me much grief over my spreadsheets), detailing clothes to wear, shoes to match, food to take, everything little thing I might need is recorded on the beloved spreadsheet. Unfortunately, life usually does not go exactly according to my plan, and my spreadsheet full of plans is blown away by circumstance, and things which are out of my control. I think the hardest part is realizing... I am not control. Well that can't be, I have planned, I have thought of everything, I have a spreadsheet! But it is true, I am not in control, and I have come to realize I am SO glad God is God and I am NOT! Initially my world caves, my plans are gone, and what do I do? It is in these moments when it's super important to be aware of how to listen to God, accept change, and chose how to respond.

Listening to God is key to understanding the direction He has for each of us, young and old. Believe me, God does have a plan. We humans usually try to intervene, to try a "shortcut", because we think we need to arrive as soon as we can, focused more on arriving then the journey. However, in the haste to cut time, ultimately we may add time or worse, we may miss something vital to our journey. This is why it is so important to seek God daily, listen to His plan, read His word to gain a better understanding of who He is so we can know who He wants us to be.

"And your ears shall hear a word behind you saying, "This is the way, walk in it", when you turn to right or to the left." Isaiah 30:21

This is God's promise to us, we will hear, He will direct us at all times! God is there, just reach out to Him in prayer, and He will direct our path. He will not leave us or forsake us, we will not be lost once we trust in Him.

I know, I know, the big question is how will I know it is God talking to me, and not just a voice in my head? Well, for me, I know God's voice because He is my father, so like my earthly father, I know His voice. I also know God will never lead me to sin, to be destructive, or to harm. God is a God of clarity not confusion, so if there is confusion, this is from Satan. God is a

God of love, so if there is not love in the direction, this also is Satan. As we continue on our journey, we do become more mature and therefore, more aware of when we are hearing God versus a lie from Satan. Remember Satan is the father of lies, he seeks to destroy us and he will lie about anything (especially Godly things) to sway us away from God. So, a good rule of thumb is this, if the voice we hear ever leads us away from God, it is of Satan, not God. God will often affirm what He is telling us through His word. He will also use other Christians in our lives to give an affirmation, or through a song, or an internal push we feel from the Holy Spirit. There are so many ways God will speak to us, we simply must be still long enough for His voice to be heard.

I went on a trip to see my mom, had my son with me. He was almost 14 at the time so my ride was silent, except for my music. You know teens; all they do is play games or sleep. Before we could get started we plugged the address into the car GPS and I started driving. Due to fires in my mom's area, she told me to make sure and travel in a certain direction so even when the GPS man kept telling me to turn around, I KNEW I needed to keep going the way I was going because my mom told me so. I do confess I am probably the only person on the planet to NOT listen to the GPS man because I know better. This is totally absurd, I mean if I knew how to get where I was going, I would not need the GPS man. Anyway, I kept driving, I just knew I needed to keep going, and then, it happened. A very large sign with flashing orange words: **Road closed due to fires.** Are you kidding me? I was beside myself, I had already driven and hour and a half, the entire way the GPS man kept telling me to turn around, but I just knew, I knew better way, so I didn't turn around, until I had to. I had lost an hour and a half plus backtracking time, so really I lost two hours, yes ladies, two hours! My drive was supposed to be six and a half hours, now I had added two hours, and that was totally dependent upon my ability to listen to GPS man in order to arrive. Sigh, I turned around. I went back the way we had already driven, and continued to my mom's house. It took a total of nine and a half hours. Turns out the GPS man knew my way was wrong, and his way was right. I just didn't want to listen, because I knew the better way. As with the GPS, I am guilty of not listening to God. I am ashamed to say, it took me years to fully trust in Him, in His plan, and in His direction for my life. It is not always easy to hear God, so often we think we have a better plan, an easier plan, a "shortcut". So we take over and ultimately end up lost, in a ditch, and end up needing God to come and save us from ourselves.

"I will instruct you and teach you in the way you should go; I will counsel you with my eye upon you." Psalm 32:8

I am reminded here of Job, this man loved God, and did all God asked, he knew God had blessed him and his family. One day Satan came to God and said, Job is only your good servant because he has everything a man could want. Would he still love and obey you if he didn't? God knew Job would still love him, so he allowed Satan to take all that was precious to Job, including his health. Job never stopped loving God. However, at times he didn't understand God's plan and why God continued to take from him that which mattered most. In the end Job was able to see God's plan. Job prayed and God blessed the later part of Job's life more than the earlier part.

"Then Job replied to the Lord; I know you can do all things; no purpose of your can be thwarted." Job 42:1

God's plan for our lives may not look like what we asked for, it might not feel good. Know this, God's plan for our life will come to pass, His way will win. We should be praying continually, for God to show us where to go and what to do each day so we make sure we are always on the right path.

God's voice will surely lead us, and His plan will not be thwarted, whether we go kicking and screaming, or quietly skipping is up to us.

ARRIVAL: ENJOY THE JOURNEY

"For I know the plans I have for you, declares the Lord, plans to prosper you and not to harm you, plans to give you hope and a future. "
Jeremiah 29:11

Isn't it great to know God is watching us? He knows where we are even when we get off the path.

"Trust in the Lord with all your heart, and do not lean on your own understanding. In all your ways acknowledge him and he will make straight your paths." Proverbs 3:5 & 6

Trust in Him and He will make straight our paths. Wow, what an awesome God we serve! Although we stray, we don't listen, and we fall, God is always with us. He will dust off the dirt, kiss this skinned knee, and tell us to keep going, He has made a way for us.

God's patience with us is unending, His mercy is new every day. Although we will often try to take a shortcut to get to where we are going, God is always there to pull us back. To get us back onto our pre-destined path. On this path God may ask us to wait, He may ask us to be still, or to change direction. In these times in our journey we need to rest in Him, in His plan, and know He is teaching us.

Paul so epitomized trusting God in times of hardship and pain. He was, after all in prison when he wrote much of the Bible. Did you know that, Paul, Jesus' disciple was imprisoned for teaching Jesus was the Son of man, for following Jesus, and for not rejecting Him? Even after being in prison for more than two years, Paul never stopped teaching about Jesus and His love. I wish I could have a tiny amount of courage that Paul had, to hang on, to continue his journey, and not be worried about how it would end (remember many disciples were killed for teaching and believe in Jesus).

We should never be so focused on arriving that we lose sight of the splendid connections, encounters, and lessons God has for us along the way. I feel sometimes we can get so laser focused on arriving at the destination we miss the beauty in the journey. Sometimes in the journey God will ask us to wait, and I will be honest here, I do not like waiting. I don't like waiting in traffic, in the line at the grocery store, or for God to answer me. I have tried to help God, and make suggestions on how to orchestrate my life so I can just get to the destination. I mean why must I wait so long? Oh thank you Lord for your grace and mercy for I do not deserve what you do for me. I have learned the hard way, the waiting is not for God, it is for me! God is using this time to sharpen me and to strengthen me for what is ahead. Waiting is not a punishment, it is preparation.

I am single and dabbled in on-line dating, which is NOT for the faint of heart. I struggled with on-line dating, not because of dating itself, but because of me. My need to feel validated and wanted was fed through on-line dating, and it quickly consumed me. I was not putting God first, I was not asking God what His plan was for my life, I was going around God to create the life I thought I wanted with men I thought I wanted to be with. To get back on track, I needed to ask God to forgive me for making a life without Him and asking God to show me the right path--His path. We are talking now about God's plan and following his path, this is true for all things in life, big or small. For those single ladies, this includes knowing if we should get involved with on-line dating. If you are married, this could mean are you humbly submitting to your husband and to God in all things, or if are you trying to "go it alone", making decisions for yourself and not including God and your husband. Whether we are single or married, one thing is true for us all, we MUST be talking to God. Ask God for guidance and direction, without this we will certainly fall.

On-line dating is a tool, like many tools invented in the world, there is both good and bad tied within it. The key is to never lose focus of where God is leading us. If God is leading us to use on-line dating, use it. But if he is not, don't. On-line dating can become obsessive, kind of like anything. Instagram, Facebook, Twitter, they are all fun and exciting, but when we spend more time on social media or on-line dating sites than with God, we are going to miss what God has for us. Let's make a promise to ourselves and to God to put Him first in our lives, to ask Him about our journey and where He wants us to go.

"Listen to me you islands; hear this, you distant nations: Before I was born the Lord called me from my mother's womb he has spoken my name. He made my mouth like a sharpened sword, in the shadow of his hand he hid me; he made me into a polished arrow and concealed me in his quiver. He said to me, "You are my servants Israel, in whom I will display my splendor. But I said. "I have labored in vain; I have spent my strength for nothing at all. Yet what is due me is in the Lord's hand and my reward is with God." Isaiah 49:1-4

We can plan, but know God is in control. This life is full of curve balls, twists, and turns. Know this ladies, God has a plan for you, He has already gone before us and prepared a way. It is up to us to seek God, in everything we do, to ask for guidance, and most importantly, we need to listen and wait. Enjoy the journey, for God is preparing us for something great. Don't worry about when you arrive, or how you will arrive; instead, focus on God and His plan for us during the journey.

It was ten years ago, I was unemployed, my ex-husband (husband at the time) was drowning in debt from the company we had started and we had four kids. What to do? How were we going to survive? I knew pretty quickly God wanted us to move to Colorado. Things fell into place, we found a place to rent, we were able to sell the house (during the recession of 2009, which was amazing itself), and we moved. I didn't have a job so things were very tight. I can remember searching and searching and nothing, no jobs. I even worked for my brother for about 6 months because we needed money. We (mostly me and the kids) started going to church. I started praying, daily. After seven months on unemployment, I finally had a job, nothing great, but it had benefits! So I took it. A few months after that, I landed the job back at the company I have been with most of my adult life.

Leaving my home in California was so hard. I cried as I was walking out and closing the front door for the last time. I had so many questions, so many worries. I was leaving everything I knew (I had grown up in California, raised my kids in California, etc.) what was going to happen now? I had no friends, no job, my oldest son (18 and in community college) decided to stay in California too, no "home". I was lost and lonely and sad, very, very sad.

Today, I have a home, all my kids live in Colorado with me, a great job, and tons of friends. But this didn't happen overnight, it took years of rebuilding, years of cultivating to rebuild. All along this journey I have had hardships (I divorced again, both my legs were broken, etc.) but I have grown more deeply in love with God, I have learned to love others the same way God loves me, I have learned to trust and hope in God, not people, for my life sustaining needs. It is the journey which provided the new beginnings, all we need to do is embrace the new possibilities, even in the valleys. Even in the darkness, even in the loneliness, knowing God has a plan, He knows what He is doing (especially when I do not).

Questions and Points to Ponder

1) What journey has God taken you on and what have you learned?

2) How will applying your ability to "enjoy" the journey help your life?

3) How has trusting in God enabled you to enjoy the journey?

CHAPTER TEN

BAGGAGE CLAIM: HOPE FOR THE FUTURE

"Jesus replied, you do not realize now what I am doing, but later you will understand."
John 13:7

December 19, 1991 Jesus gave me strength and courage beyond what I was capable of dealing with on my own. In His strength and courage, I was able to leave my daughter with her parents and leave the hospital. A few months later God also gave me to opportunity to see my daughter, to know she was okay. My circumstances allowed me to see or obtain proof my daughter was doing well, but what about the times we don't see, when we don't know what God is doing?

John 13:7 tells us that we will not always have proof; we will not always know what He is doing in our lives because He wants us to trust in Him, to have faith in Him. He will reveal His plan, His work in His timing, when He knows we are ready to understand. We need to have hope, in God, in God's plan for our future, and in waiting for God's timing.

It was probably 2005 (Can't remember the exact date, and I didn't write miracles down back then) and I had been going back to church and a bible study and I had started praying again, specifically about my daughter. It had been fourteen years since I had seen her and I really, really, really wanted to know how she was. So I started asking God to let know how she was, what I most wanted was to see her. Almost like when she was four months old, I needed proof she was still okay. So, I prayed, and prayed. No answer for many months, then one day, I am at a park with my daughter who was born a few years after the one I gave up for adoption. She was at cheer practice, I had my youngest son with me as well, he was about a year old. He was doing what boys do, sitting in the dirt in the baseball dug out playing. I was standing there watching him and I hear this voice behind me yell "Hey mom!" Well you know how it is ladies when you hear "mom" you instinctively turn, it's just what we do. I turned and directly behind me, not more than an arms-length away, was my daughter. All grown up, fourteen years old. I was so close, she was right there, and I looked up and there was her mom. There are no words to describe my feelings at that moment. I wanted to hug her, but it was not my place. I wanted to kiss her cheek but it was not my place. God put us together, on that day, in that park, in that moment, so I could again see my daughter was good. It was not time for a reunion, not yet at least. In a matter of seconds she was gone, walking away with her mom and my son stated crying, so I went to pick him up. I scooped him up and kissed him and hugged him so tight. I was shaking. I knew what just happened, I knew God made that moment happen, I knew God was with me. God answered my prayer, in a way I would never have conceived.

"This is the confidence we have in approaching God: that if we ask anything according to his will, he hears us. And if we know that he hears us- whatever we ask – we know that we have what we asked for."
I John 5:14 & 15

Ladies, God is working in our lives, even when, especially when, we don't see. We should boldly, confidently approach God in prayer, asking for healing, asking for guidance, asking for wisdom, and making requests. I did, and look at what He did, how amazing is our God! He loves us so much He did that for me, for *me*. Wow, when I think about that day, I am always both terrified and amazed by God, His power, and His love for me.

From the time I gave my daughter to her parents, one of my greatest hopes was she and her brother (who was a year older than her), would one day meet one another. After all, they are full brother and sister. I wanted them to know they had each other, and I always told my son about her, so he would know she was out there, and secretly I hoped they would search for each other and find each other later in life. Siblings are so important, knowing you have a full blood sibling was important to me.

I'll be honest here; I can't say I ever prayed for a reunion between siblings, I simply had a hope in my heart. I am here to tell you ladies, a simple hope is enough.

"In the same way the Spirit helps us in our weakness. We do not know what we ought to pray for, but the Spirit himself intercedes for us through wordless groans. And he who searches our hearts knows the mind of the Spirit, because the Spirit intercedes for God's people in accordance with the will of God."
Romans 8:26 &27

God is so wonderful, He thought of everything we might ever need and graciously, mercifully gave, yes gave it all to us. His Spirit lives in us. Let that sink in, the Spirit of God lives in each of us. His Spirit is part of us, He hears us when we don't speak aloud, and His Spirit knows what we need before we can even ask. He knows how to plead for us when we don't know what to say. To say God is good is such an understatement.

"Do not be like them, for your Father knows what you need before you ask."
Matthew 6:8

117

In summer 2007 I was at work, just a regular, ordinary day at work, but this day would change my life (again). God has a way of taking the regular, ordinary and making something so special. I was driving home from work and I receive a call, unknown number, so of course, I didn't answer. I mean who answers unknown numbers?

The person left a voice message, when I listened, I could not believe what I was hearing. The call was from my adoption counselor and she advised me my daughter wanted to meet me, but her parents wanted to meet with me first. Would I be interested? If so please return her call. It felt like someone else's life, like I was having an out of body experience. My daughter wanted to meet me. Wow. There were so many thoughts going through my head, I could hardly think straight. I was shaking, but I called her right back, spoke with her, and set up a time to meet with her parents.

The day I was to meet her parents I felt lost, nervous, sick to my stomach. What if they didn't like me? What if they said I couldn't meet my daughter? What if? What if? What if? I was in knots, going crazy in my head. My hands were shaking so bad I couldn't drive, my mind was racing. Then I was there, I think we shook hands (remember, my mind was not clear, so I don't recall every detail). We sat and started talking. It was so wonderful, so great; we decided to plan a date to have our families meet.

We met in the park behind my house, under a large tree. I had all my kids and my husband (I was still married in 2007). My daughter had her parents, grandparents, and her brother. When I first saw her it was hard for me to contain my feelings. I wanted to run to her and hug her and kiss her, but I didn't want to scare her off, so I decided to take it slow. I walked up to her, we hugged, for a brief moment, nothing too intense. I also hugged her parents and grandparents; we did introductions and started talking.

Remember back to what one of greatest hopes were, that my son and daughter would one day know each other? Well, God did something so powerful, so wonderful, it is hard to put into words. As we sat there in the park, talking, we learned that my daughter's mom (her parents had divorced) lived in a house less than two miles from mine. They had lived in that house since 1996 and I had lived in mine since 1997. My daughter and son went to middle school and high school together, they knew each other! My other daughter and my adopted daughter ate lunch at the same lunch table in high school. We had never seen each other, except the one occasion in 2005 at the park. In the eight years we lived that close, we never were in the same grocery store or gas station or restaurant, ever, not until God said, it is time. I didn't pray for a reunion, I never prayed that my kids would know each other; it was a simple hope in my heart. God knew, God always knew, because it was His plan.

God was working, He was working hard ladies! I mean how it is possible we lived that close for so many years and never once came into contact with each other (except when designed by God)? I don't believe in coincidence. I believe in "Godsidence" meaning there are no accidental, arbitrary incidents in life. God has every step, every move, every incident planned and He already knows the outcome. He knows the ending, even when we can't see the forest through the trees, He knows.

Listen ladies, God is working, even when, especially when we don't see "behind the scene." He is always working. We can never give up, we can never lose hope. God is our hope. God is our hope for the future.

I could never have imagined meeting my daughter, much less learning how God orchestrated our lives so meticulously to keep us from each other but allow the kids to know one another. To be around one another, and to live so close to one another. A side note, my daughter has a brother, and he was born on the same day, within hours, of my second son's birth (almost like twins, but from separate/same families). Again, absolutely supercalafragalistically awesome!

So, when you are at the end, when you don't see the light in your darkness. When you lose someone special, when you don't get that job you wanted, when your husband leaves for another woman, when your kid gets arrested, when your grandchild is strung out on drugs, when you lose your home, your car stops running, when the pain and hurts of yesterday are overwhelming you, when you can't see the proof God is working because it looks like God isn't even around: Keep going, don't give up.

I know you are asking, but how? How can I keep going? I can't even get out of bed today. Here is how: take the first step. Even if it is simply getting out of bed, get out of bed. Do this for awhile, then add another step, get out of bed, and go for a walk. The point is to keep moving, taking baby steps until you can take bigger steps, but keep moving, keep trusting in God, keep hope alive in the little things each day. This is not easy, nor is it fast. We are human, therefore, we need time to reflect. Time to be angry, time to be sad, and time to heal. Healing is a process, but I promise, once we start God is there, providing exactly who and what we need for each day. I know this may not seem true, but I am asking you to trust, believe, hope.

Hour by hour, day by day, week by week, month by month, keep moving, keeping taking steps, God is with us, God is with you, keep the faith!

> *God is working, even when, especially when, we don't see "behind the scenes."*

In the darkest times remember this story. Remember your story. Remember when He pulled you out from the ditch, from the valley of darkness we were all in before coming to Him. Know He is with you, He will never leave you, or forsake you, and He is in you. He has already paid the price for us. He died and rose again! He is not punishing us, He is preparing us, for the great plan He has for our lives.

We know after the darkness of night we will wake to the light of a new day. Such is true in our lives, there are ebbs and flows in life. We must choose to hold out for the light of a new day, to not give up. To live our best life each day, knowing God is with us in the darkness and in the light.

Trust in him, always and forever.

Ladies, the tiniest hope in our heart is known by God. He can see into us because He is in us. All we need to do is believe in Him, receive Him, and live for Him.

As I sit here recounting this story, looking out my office window at the birds, I am reminded of how powerful and great our God is. His great power lives in us, in me. He is so powerful He makes sure the birds have a food, every single day. They do not worry for they know food will be there, the birds just know, there is no room for worry and doubt. How great would that be to never worry or doubt that God will provide? We can, we can chose to live in God's promise, we can chose to live like the birds and not worry or doubt, just believe.

This ride has been bumpy, full of ups and downs. God's story in my life brought me through a suicide attempt, an eating disorder, adoption, medical set-backs, job loss, moving, financial loss and instability, two unsuccessful marriages, countless failed relationships, and I am sure there is more to come. But I am choosing today, right now, to live like the birds. To cling to my hope in God, to never worry or doubt, knowing, believing God is my provider, my protector, my everything. He gave His life for me. The greatest gift we have is the life, death, and resurrection of Jesus. Cling tight to this gift, for through this we can live our lives in hope. Hope for our future and both here on this earth, and one day in heaven.

We need to take our baggage claim tickets and give them to God, once and for all. We need to leave our baggage behind. We need to lay our baggage at the feet of God, and trust He will take our bags releasing us from the strain and heaviness of our past, and feeing us to take our future, filled with faith, hope, and love.

The tiniest hope in our heart is known by God, He can see into us because He is in us.

Questions and Points to Ponder

1) When was a time God was working in your life, but you were not aware until later?

2) How will you take the first step?

3) How can you cling to God in the darkest places?

4) How can you begin to hope in your future?

5) How can you keep trusting in God, in the valley?

6) How can you be a woman of righteousness?

We are Women Of Righteousness Through Him

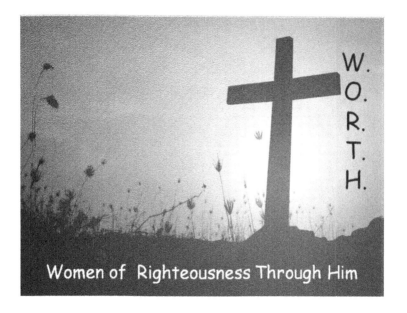

Made in the USA
Monee, IL
31 October 2021